Muslims Jews Christians

Defeating Hate

A
Comprehensive
Rebuttal of Taliban, AlQaeda, Daesh (ISIS)
and Islamophobes

Syed Badiuddin Soharwardy

Islamic Supreme Council of Canada
Muslims Against Terrorism

ISBN 978-1-68418-051-6

This book is dedicated to Prophet Muhammad (Peace be upon him), the perfect model for everyone to follow, the final Messenger of God towards humanity and the receiver of the complete guidance from Allah – the Holy Qur'an. He is my ideal, hero and guide. I hope I will have the opportunity to kiss his feet when I meet him on the Judgement Day. O' Allah's Messenger I love you from the bottom of my heart.

I pray to almighty Allah to bless my parents with His mercy and forgiveness. They raised me and my brothers and sisters with good education and utmost care and love under very difficult living conditions. May Allah bless them with the intercession of Prophet Muhammad (peace be upon him) on the Judgement Day.

This book is a result of constant and consistence guidance that I receive from my father, teacher and spiritual guide (Murshid) Hazrat Allama Syed Muhammad Riazuddin Soharwardy (May Allah's mercy on him). He passed away in 2001 but we are still in touch.

I am very thankful to my wife, daughter and son for their sacrifices and support. I use my family's time to serve my faith, my community and the country. Without my family's support I could not have achieved what I have achieved.

I am grateful to Linda Zachri for proof reading this book. I am thankful to Masood Ahmed Qadri, Ali Shah, Zahid Rafique Soharwardy and Muhammad Rehan Soharwardy for their help in getting this book printed. May Allah reward all of them.

I am very thankful to Brother Nehal Syed for providing financial support for the second edition to be printed sooner than expected due to the huge demand for this book. May Allah reward Brother Nehal Syed for his support.

JazakAllah.

Preface

In this competitive, highly technology-based world, the accuracy of information, and maintaining this information, has become a serious issue. Information is the major asset of a society; however, an abundance of information on a given subject, is not necessarily an indicator that the information is correct. We are living in the "information age", which has both good and bad effects on society. The new technology based communication tools of the internet and email have changed the world forever. Now it has become very difficult for ordinary people to separate inaccurate "information" from accurate information. Animosity, jealousy and special interests have all played a role in moving people to fabricate information about their opponents and to spread these fabrications instantaneously. The main objective of this book is twofold: to respond to the false information, spread by the extremists and terrorists using Islam to misguide and recruit Muslim youth to their causes, and to refute the Islamophobes whose attacks on Islam serve to create more terrorists.

After the tragedy of 9/11, two new business industries emerged in the world, Security & Safety and Islamophobia. The safety and security industry depends on Islamophobia for growth. The Islamophobia industry manufactures lies and spreads rumors about Islam and Muslims. Hundreds of Islamophobic websites misquote or even create incorrect translations of the verses of the Holy Qur'an. These websites have confused thousands of people in the world, especially the western world, about Islam, Muslims and the Qur'an. This book is intended as both a rebuttal of Islamophobic propaganda, and a clear condemnation of organizations like Daesh (ISIS), Al-Qaedah, Taliban, Boko Haram, Al Nusrah, Al Shabab, Lashkar Taiba, Lashkar Jhangwi, etc. Its purpose is to provide its readers with an authentic, logical, rational context of those very verses of the Qur'an liberally quoted by Islamophobes and the terrorists in their effort to "prove" that the Qur'an is a book of hate, and that Muslims hate Jews, Christians, infidels, non-Muslims, non-believers, and so on.

I N D E X

Part I

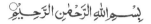

In the Name of Allah, the Most Compassionate the Most Merciful

Introduction

In order to understand the Qur'an, it is essential to understand the basics of Qur'anic science. The Qur'an was revealed to the Prophet Muhammad (Peace be upon him) over a span of almost 23 years. There are two types of verses in the Qur'an; Muta-sha-bihat (metaphoric) and Moh-kamat (clear). Only a very small number of verses are metaphoric. The overwhelming majority of Qur'anic verses are Mohkam (clear). These Mohkam verses deal with subjects that include beliefs, deeds, laws, guidance, history, stories, dealings, business and human relationships. Out of this 23-year period of revelation (Wahee), the Prophet Muhammad (PBUH) and his followers lived 13 years in Makkah under persecution and 10 years in Madinah in relatively easier circumstances, but still under constant threat and periodic attacks from pagans and other non-Muslims. The Prophet Muhammad (PBUH) started receiving revelations (Wahee) at the age of 40. He was born in Makkah. He migrated to Madinah at the age of 53. He passed away in Madinah when he was 63.

Most of the time WAHEE (revelations) from Allah (God) came to Prophet Muhammad (PBUH) based upon the events and the incidents that took place during the 23 years mentioned earlier. Someone asked a question, Allah sent His guidance in the form of verses of the holy Qur'an, and the Prophet (PBUH) answered the question. Something happened, Allah sent a revelation. Something was going to happen. Allah informed the Prophet Muhammad (PBUH) about it. So, most of the verses of the holy Qur'an are not intended to be understood in isolation, but in context. Sometimes this context can be found within the Qur'an itself, and sometimes other sources must be referred to. In order to fully understand the meaning of a verse, knowledge of the context is mandatory. Another important source for understanding Qur'anic verses is the knowledge of how Prophet Muhammad (PBUH) himself understood and acted according to those same verses, and how his companions (Sahabah) and his family members (Ahlul Bait) understood and acted according to the verses. We cannot just take the verses literally and claim that we understand them. The most important factor involved in a correct understanding of the verses of the holy Qur'an is an understanding of the personality of Prophet Muhammad (PBUH), based upon his characteristics, qualities, morals and dealings mentioned in the holy Qur'an. This is the key point which has the potential to lead, not only non-Muslims, but many Muslims to make mistakes in Qur'anic exegesis.

To correctly understand the meaning of the verses of the holy Qur'an, one must be acquainted with the style of Qur'an. An insufficient understanding of the style of the holy Qur'an leads inevitably to a deficiency in the understanding of the Qur'an itself. Sometimes a passage in the Qur'an talks in very general terms about a person, a group of people, or an event, but the application of the passage is meant to apply to a very specific person, people or event. These are the types of verses that Islamophobes misquote in order to confuse people about Islam and Muslims. Ironically, these are also the verses that the hatemongers, terrorists and extremists use to incite hate towards Jews, Christians and others who oppose them, including other Muslims as well as non-Muslims. It is hugely dishonest to select a verse of the Qur'an to justify a point of view while completely ignoring the other related verses. Following cases describe the reasons of misunderstanding.

Case 1: Reading a verse in isolation and ignoring its link with other verse(s).

In the following verse Muslim worshipers are addressed. The verse has nothing to do with non-Muslims.

Qur'an: "So woe to the worshippers" (107:4)

Apparently in this verse, Allah is cursing Muslim worshipers. However, no Muslim believes that Allah is cursing ALL Muslim worshipers. Worship is an integral part of Muslim life. Now read the next verses.

Qur'an: "Who are neglectful of their Prayers. Those who (want but) to be seen (of men). But refuse (to supply) (Even) neighbourly needs." (107:5,6,7)

A reading of the next verses reveals that the woe is for specific Muslims, not all Muslims. However, verse 4 of Surah 107, read in isolation, appears to curse all worshipers. It is imperative to read the other related verses to understand the full meaning and the message; whereas, reading verses in isolation from other related verses can lead to an entirely different understanding.

Here is another example to illustrate the previous point. A reading of the following three verses in the 26th chapter, Surah Al Sho'ara, can lead to the conclusion that the Qur'an unequivocally condemns all poets.

Qur'an: "And the Poets— it is those straying in Evil, who follow them. Seest thou not that they wander distracted in every valley? And that they say what they practise not?" (26: 224, 225, 226)

However, it is very well known and a historical fact that several Companions of Prophet Muhammad (PBUH) were poets. The poetry of those companions are still safe and available in books for anyone to read. The poetry of Hazrat Abu Bakr, Hazrat Omar, Hazrat Imam Ali, Sayyidah Fatemah Al Zahra, Sayyida Aisha Siddiqah, Hazrat Hassaan Ibn Thabit, Hazrat Abdullah Ibn Rawaha (May Allah's peace and blessings upon all of them), and other heroes of Islam, is readily available. Are these noble companions and the family members of Prophet Muhammad (PBUH) in the above mentioned verses included? When does Allah not like poets why did these noble Muslims continue to write poetry right in the presence of Prophet Muhammad (PBUH)? The answer is that Allah does not forbid all types of poetry. Allah does not condemn all poets. In order to understand the entire scenario, we have to read the next verses, too.

Qur'an: "Except those who believe, work righteousness, engage much in the remembrance of Allah, and defend themselves after they are unjustly attacked. And soon will the unjust assailants know what vicissitudes their affairs will take!" (26: 227)

A reading of verse 227 from the same Surah clarifies the guidance and proves that Allah likes poets who are honest in their poetry. But both Islamophobes and terrorists pick and choose verses of Qur'an which they can quote to confuse and misguide people while ignoring the other related verses. A few years ago in Calgary, a Muslim Imam with a Ph.D. from Saudi Arabia quoted verses 224-226 of Surah 26 only and ignored verse 227 in order to "prove" his view on poetry which praises Prophet Muhammad (PBUH). Such poetry is called "Naat". Since he did not like Naat, he chose only those verses which appeared to match his beliefs or agenda, and ignored the other related verse which could have contradicted him.

Case 2: Apparently Broad Verses, but with a Very Specific Application

There are several verses in the holy Qur'an which describe a group of people or an event in what appears to be very broad, general terms; nevertheless, those verses cannot be taken as literally "general". They should really be applied to very specific people. Here are some examples of those verses.

> ***Qur'an:*** *Man is created weak (4: 28)*

> ***Qur'an:*** *We did indeed offer the Trust to the Heavens and the Earth and the Mountains: but they refused to undertake it, being afraid thereof: but man undertook it— he was indeed unjust and foolish (33: 72)*

> ***Qur'an:*** *He has* created man *from a sperm-drop; and behold this same (*man*) becomes an open disputer! (16: 4)*

> ***Qur'an:*** *Truly* man *was* created *very impatient; - (70: 19)*

> ***Qur'an:*** *The prayer that* man *should make for good, he maketh for evil; for* man *is given to* hasty *(deeds). (17: 11)*

> ***Qur'an:*** *Verily Allah will not deal unjustly with man in aught: It is man that wrongs his own soul. (10: 44)*

After reading the above several verses from various parts of the holy Qur'an, what is one to conclude? The Qur'an says humans are weak, unjust, foolish, disputers, impatient, hasty, wrongdoers, and so on. Does this mean the Qur'an hates and insults humans? Of course, not!

One of the core beliefs of Islam is that all the Prophets and the Messengers of Allah were human, including the Prophet Muhammad himself (PBUH). Moreover, the Family (Ahlul Bait) and the Companions (Sahabah) of Prophet Muhammad (PBUH), Saints (Aulia Allah), the true believers (Mo'mineen) and righteous Muslims (Saleheen) are praised in the holy Qur'an hundreds of times and given the good news of Heaven by Allah. All these people were humans, too. So the above verses should never be interpreted to include the prophets, saints and righteous Muslims as being among the weak, the unjust, foolish, the disputers, the impatient, the hasty, the wrongdoers and other transgressors. We exclude these humans from those verses, even though they seem to be addressing all human beings. The verses may seem all-inclusive, but exceptions must be considered.

Case 3: Muslims are Condemned, Too

Allah condemns anyone who disobeys Allah's guidance. This includes Muslims. The following verses refer only to Muslims. Non-Muslims are not addressed here.

> *Qur'an: These are the limits (imposed by) Allah. Transgress them not. For whoso transgresseth Allah's limits: such are wrong-doers. (2: 229)*

> *Qur'an: Those who after receiving direction from their Lord, desist, shall be pardoned for the past; their case is for Allah (to judge); but those who repeat (the offence) are companions of the Fire: they will abide therein (forever). (2: 275)*

> *Qur'an: By no means shall ye attain righteousness unless ye give (freely) of that which ye love; and whatever ye give, Allah knoweth it well. (3: 92)*

Qur'an: *Those who unjustly eat up the property of orphans, eat up a Fire into their own bodies: they will soon be enduring a blazing Fire!* *(4: 10)*

Qur'an: *But those who disobey Allah and His Messenger and transgress His limits will be admitted to a Fire to abide therein: and they shall have a humiliating punishment.* *(4: 14)*

Qur'an: *If any do fail to judge by (the light of) what Allah hath revealed, they are (no better than) Unbelievers.* *(5: 44)*

Qur'an: *And if any fail to judge by (the light of) what Allah hath revealed, they are (no better than) wrongdoers.* *(5: 45)*

Qur'an: *If any do fail to judge by (the light of) what Allah hath revealed, they are (no better than) those who rebel.* *(5: 47)*

Qur'an: *O ye who believe! Make not unlawful the good things which Allah hath made lawful for you but commit no excess: for Allah loveth not those given to excess.* *(5: 87)*

There are hundreds of similar verses in the holy Qur'an warning Muslims about the wrath of Allah that will come down on those "Muslims" who do not follow the guidance of the Qur'an and the Prophet Muhammad (PBUH) in various issues and matters of life. But no Muslim believes that Allah hates all Muslims.

Case 4: Allah Declares War against Muslims

I could not find any verse in the holy Qur'an with such strong, frightening words for anyone. This verse refers only to Muslims, and has nothing to do with any non-Muslims.

Qur'an: *If ye do it not, take notice of war from Allah and His Messenger...* *(2:279)*

After usury was prohibited in Islam Muslims were warned that if they continued to practice usury in their lending and borrowing businesses, they would face a challenge of war from almighty Allah and His Messenger (PBUH). After reading a challenge of war to Muslims from Allah does anyone believe the Qur'an hates Muslims? Of course no one believes that.

Similarly, the following verse applies to both Muslims and non-Muslims alike but one may conclude the Qur'an is condemning non-Muslims.

> *Qur'an: If then they turn away, We have not sent thee as a guard over them. Thy duty is but to convey (the Message). And truly when We give man a taste of Mercy from Ourselves he doth exult thereat, but when some ill happens to him, on account of the deeds which His hands have sent forth, truly then is man ungrateful! (42:48)*

The above four cases give you some understanding of Qur'an's style of addressing certain issues or guidance. These verses cannot be considered harsh, hateful or violent verses against all humans, poets and Muslims, although a superficial reading of the translation could make these verses appear that way. Please keep these four cases in mind in order to understand the next verses. We will now analyze those verses of Qur'an which Islamophobes quote to "prove" that the Qur'an hates Jews, Christians or non-Muslims, and that terrorist organizations use to recruit people in order to create violence against non-Muslims.

Pagans, Jews and Christians

> *Qur'an: And well ye knew those amongst you who transgressed in the matter of the Sabbath; We said to them: "Be ye apes despised and rejected." (2:65)*

> *Qur'an: Say: "O People of the Book! do ye disapprove of us for no other reason than that we believe in Allah, and the revelation that hath come to us and that which came before (us), and (perhaps) that most of you are rebellious and disobedient?" Say: "Shall I point out to you something much worse than this, (as judged) by the treatment it received from Allah? Those who incurred the curse of Allah and His wrath, those of whom some*

He transformed into apes and swine, those who worshipped Evil;— these are (many times) worse in rank and far more astray from the even Path! (5:59-60)

Qur'an: *"When in their insolence they transgressed (all) prohibition, We said to them: "Be ye apes, despised and rejected." (7:166)*

The above verses from Qur'an cannot be generalized for all Jews. They are very specific about those people who disobeyed God's commandments, and were punished by God for their disobedience. No hate is implied here against Jews in general, as the same sort of disobedience is also condemned in the holy Bible. Consider the following Biblical verses.

Bible: *"While the Israelites were in the wilderness, a man was found gathering wood on the Sabbath day. Those who found him gathering wood brought him to Moses and Aaron and the whole assembly, and they kept him in custody, because it was not clear what should be done to him. Then the LORD said to Moses, "The man must die. The whole assembly must stone him outside the camp." So the assembly took him outside the camp and stoned him to death, as the LORD commanded Moses." (Bible, Numbers 15:32-36).*

Bible: *Observe the Sabbath, because it is holy to you. Anyone who desecrates it is to be put to death; those who do any work on that day must be cut off from their people. [15] For six days work is to be done, but the seventh day is a day of Sabbath rest, holy to the LORD. Whoever does any work on the Sabbath day is to be put to death. (Bible, Exodus 31:14-15)*

I leave it to you to decide which one is more threatening, the verse from the Qur'an, or the Bible? At least the Qur'an does not demand the death penalty for violating the Sabbath.

Obviously the above verses from the Qur'an and the Bible are very specific to those Jews who disobeyed Allah's guidance in the Torah. These verses cannot and should not be generalized for all Jews. Allah repeatedly condemns those Muslims who disobey Him. As this does not mean Allah does not like all Muslims, the same reasoning applies to Jews as well.

> ***Qur'an:*** *And when there comes to them a Book from Allah, confirming what is with them. —although from of old they had prayed for victory against those without faith —when there comes to them that which they (should) have recognized, they refuse to believe in it; but the curse of Allah is on those without Faith. (2:89)*

What does the Bible say about the same people?

> ***Bible:*** *Obey my laws and teachings. Or else the land I am giving you will become sick of you and throw you out. The nations I am chasing out did these disgusting things, and I hated them for it, so don't follow their example. (Leviticus, 20:22-23)*

> ***Bible:*** *But it shall come about, if you do not obey the LORD your God, to observe to do all His commandments and His statutes with which I charge you today, that all these curses will come upon you and overtake you: (Deuteronomy, 28:15)*

The Qur'anic and Biblical verses both make it obvious that God warns people about His wrath if people disobey His commandments. Those people could be Jewish, Christians OR Muslims. The Qur'an does not specify Jews and Christians only. As with the Bible, this aspect of the Qur'an is directed towards everyone who does not follow God's commandments.

Relationships with Jews and Christians

> ***Qur'an:*** *Let not the Believers take for friends or helpers unbelievers rather than believers; if any do that, shall*

have no relation left with Allah except by way of precaution, that ye may guard yourselves from them. But Allah cautions you (to fear) Himself for the final goal is to Allah. (3:28)

Qur'an: *O ye who believe! take not the Jews and the Christians for your friends and protectors: they are but friends and protectors to each other. And he amongst you that turns to them (for friendship) is of them. Verily Allah guideth not a people unjust. (5:51)*

Qur'an: *"Muhammad is the Messenger of Allah, and those who are with him are hard against the unbelievers, merciful one to another." (48:29).*

Once again we see verses that appear to be general in nature but, again refer to a very specific guidance. Additional verses along those lines in the holy Qur'an are also not there to promote hate or discrimination against non-Muslim individuals. The above verses, and many similar verses, describe the criteria of foreign policy of a Muslim government; the relationships with other countries, trade, tariffs, intelligence sharing, defense and security arrangements. Is it possible for the American government to establish similar levels of trade, relationships, defense, security and intelligence sharing with Pakistan, Saudi Arabia, Sudan to those which America has with Canada? No reasonable person would say so. This is not because America discriminates against Pakistan, Saudi Arabia, Sudan. It is simply natural and normal for the relationships between Canada and the United States to be closer, stronger and more cordial than the relationship between the United States and the other three aforementioned countries. Canada and the United States share thousands of miles of a common border. In addition, these two countries have many commonalities in the areas of culture, history, systems, interests and other factors.

Similarly, the Qur'an provides guidance to a Muslim government to the effect that its foreign policy should also be based upon common borders, cultures, systems and interests. It does not teach hate or discrimination towards anyone. Just because it is easier for an American citizen to get a Canadian visitor's visa than it is for a Rwandan, Eritrean or Ugandan citizen, does this mean Canada is unfairly restrictive towards the citizens of these last three countries? Off course not. It's all about comfort zones and relationships, and should not be considered hateful or discriminatory. The above verses guided the newly-born Islamic country of Madinah fourteen centuries ago to have closer ties and relationships with those tribes and countries which were closer, than with those not as close. It does not mean that Muslim countries should not have any relationship with the Jewish or Christian countries. The verse is about the foreign policy of a Muslim country, not about the behaviour of individuals. Unfortunately, today almost all Muslim governments have avoided this guidance of the holy Qur'an, and every Muslim country aspires to having friendliest relationships with America, instead of friendliest relationship among themselves.

Let us review some of the important evidence from the life of the Prophet Muhammad (PBUH) showing the relationships with non-Muslims, including pagans, Jews and Christians.

Hilful Fodhul: Tribal wars were very common among Arabs and used to last for centuries. A similar tribal war was going on in Arabia among several tribes for a very long time. This war ended due to the efforts of Prophet Muhammad (PBUH). He negotiated an agreement among various pagan tribes during the 7th century to end the war. The agreement is called Hilful Fodhul. It ended several years of wars among various pagan tribes of Makkah and peace was established for all the pagans. According to this agreement, human rights of all citizens were respected.

The Covenant of Madinah (Mithaq-e-Madinah): This was an agreement among the Muslims, Jews and pagans of Madinah, and was also initiated and brokered by Prophet Muhammad (PBUH). The covenant of Madinah was the first agreement that established the rule of law and equal human rights for all Muslims and non-Muslims in the newly created Islamic country of Madinah. This covenant clearly defined the loyalty with the state with complete religious freedom for all faith groups in

Madinah. It established the principles of national unity among the citizens of the state. The covenant clearly said that the Jews would have the full support from Muslims if they faced any threat from anyone. Any assault on non-Muslims would be treated as an assault on Muslims. The covenant also said that the Jews shall be treated along with the believers as one community, with the Jews having their own religion and the Muslims having their own religion; and that this shall apply to them and their freedmen [i.e., allies], with the exception of those who act unjustly or sinfully. "The Jews shall bear their expenses and Muslims shall bear theirs" asserts the principle of economic solidarity when distributing economic responsibilities among the different groups in society. "They shall render support against anyone who fights any party to this pact" and "They shall owe it to each other to give mutual sincere counsel." [Dr. John Andrew Morrow, *The Covenants of the Prophet Muhammad,* Angelico Press, 2013]

Letter to the Monks of St. Catherine Monastery: The historic letter from Prophet Muhammad (PBUH) himself to the Christian monks of St. Catherine is the most authentic bases for Christian-Muslim relationships. Here is the letter translated in English.

"This is a letter which was issued by Mohammed, Ibn Abdullah, the Messenger, the Prophet, the Faithful, who is sent to all the people as a trust on the part of God to all His creatures, that they may have no plea against God hereafter. Verily God is the Mighty, the Wise. This letter is directed to the embracers of Islam, as a covenant given to the followers of Jesus the Nazarene in the East and West, the far and near, the Arabs and foreigners, the known and the unknown.

This letter contains the oath given unto them, and he who disobeys that which is therein will be considered a disobeyer and a transgressor to that whereunto he is commanded. He will be regarded as one who has corrupted the oath of God, disbelieved His Testament, rejected His Authority, despised His Religion, and made himself deserving of His Curse, whether he is a Sultan or any other believer of Islam. Whenever Christian monks, devotees and pilgrims gather together, whether in a mountain or valley, or den, or frequented place, or plain, or church, or in houses of worship, verily we are [at the] back of them and shall protect them, and their properties and their morals, by Myself, by My Friends and by My Assistants, for they are of My Subjects and under My Protection.

I shall exempt them from that which may disturb them; of the burdens which are paid by others as an oath of allegiance. They must not give anything of their income but that which pleases them—they must not be offended, or disturbed, or coerced or compelled. Their judges should not be changed or prevented from accomplishing their offices, nor the monks disturbed in exercising their religious order, or the people of seclusion be stopped from dwelling in their cells.

No one is allowed to plunder these Christians, or destroy or spoil any of their churches, or houses of worship, or take any of the things contained within these houses and bring it to the houses of Islam. And he who takes away anything therefrom, will be one who has corrupted the oath of God, and, in truth, disobeyed His Messenger.

Jizya should not be put upon their judges, monks, and those whose occupation is the worship of God; nor is any other thing to be taken from them, whether it be a fine, a tax or any unjust right. Verily I shall keep their compact, wherever they may be, in the sea or on the land, in the East or West, in the North or South, for they are under My Protection and the testament of My Safety, against all things which they abhor.

No taxes or tithes should be received from those who devote themselves to the worship of God in the mountains, or from those who cultivate the Holy Lands. No one has the right to interfere with their affairs, or bring any action against them. Verily this is for aught else and not for them; rather, in the seasons of crops, they should be given a Kadah for each Ardab of wheat (about five bushels and a half) as provision for them, and no one has the right to say to them this is too much, or ask them to pay any tax.

As to those who possess properties, the wealthy and merchants, the poll-tax to be taken from them must not exceed twelve drachmas a head per year (i.e. the equivalent of about 200 US dollars).

They shall not be imposed upon by anyone to undertake a journey, or to be forced to go to wars or to carry arms; for the Muslims have to fight for them. Do no dispute or argue with them, but deal according to the verse recorded in the Koran, to wit: 'Do not dispute or argue with the People of the Book but in that which is best' [29:46]. Thus they will live favored and protected from everything which may offend them by the Callers to religion (Islam), wherever they may be and in any place they may dwell.

Should any Christian woman be married to a Muslim, such marriage must not take place except after her consent, and she must not be prevented from going to her church for prayer. Their churches must be honored and they must not be withheld from building churches or repairing convents.

They must not be forced to carry arms or stones; but the Muslims must protect them and defend them against others. It is positively incumbent upon every one of the Islam nation not to contradict or disobey this oath until the Day of Resurrection and the end of the world." (Haddad, Anton F., trans. The Oath of the Prophet Mohammed to the Followers of the Nazarene. New York: Board of Counsel, 1902; H-Vahabi: Lansing, MI: 2004)

What other evidence do these Islamophobes and the terrorists need from Islam? Muslims are required by our faith not to hate or discriminate against Christians. In fact, it is the requirement of our Faith to protect the lives and properties of Christians living in an Islamic country. Why are the Islamophobes unable find verses like the following in the holy Qur'an about Jews and Christians?

> *Qur'an: Not all of them are alike: of the People of the book are a portion that stand (for the right); they rehearse the signs of Allah all night long, and they prostrate themselves in adoration. They believe in*

Allah and the Last Day; they enjoin what is right, and forbid what is wrong; and they hasten (in emulation) in (all) good works; they are in the ranks of the righteous. Of the good that they do, nothing will be rejected of them; for Allah knoweth well those that do right. (3:113-115)

During the early days of Islam in Makkah, pagans came to the Prophet Muhammad (PBUH) and bragged about the victory of the Persians (fire / Sun worshipers) over the Romans (Christians). The pagans were closer to the Persians in terms of their beliefs, which is why they always sided with the Persians whenever a conflict took place between Persians and Romans. However, when a pagan came to the Messenger of Allah (PBUH) and wanted to test his prophesy about the war between the Persians and the Romans, The Prophet (PBUH) took the side of Romans as Allah guided him. He told the pagans that the next victory would be Roman. And in next war between Persians and Romans, this came to pass as it was promised by Allah in the holy Qur'an.

> ***Qur'an:*** *The Roman Empire has been defeated— In a land close by; but they, (even) after (this) defeat of theirs, will soon be victorious. Within a few years. With Allah is the Decision, in the Past and in the Future: on that Day shall the Believers rejoice— With the help of Allah. He helps whom He will, and He is Exalted in Might, Most Merciful. (It is) the promise of Allah. Never does Allah depart from His promise: but most men understand not. (30:2-6)*

These verses again prove that the holy Qur'an wishes good to Christians and that there is no hate towards them.

Superiority

> ***Qur'an:*** *Ye are the best of peoples, evolved for mankind, enjoining what is right, forbidding what is wrong, and believing in Allah. If only the People of the Book had faith it were best for them; among them are some who have faith, but most of them are perverted transgressors. (3:110)*

Islamophobes quote the above verse from Qur'an to prove that Qur'an considers Muslims superior over non-Muslims. Let's see do we have similar verse in Bible about Jews?

Bible: for you are a people holy to the LORD your God. Out of all the peoples on the face of the earth, the LORD has chosen you to be his treasured possession. (Deuteronomy 14:2)

Should Muslims be offended by the above verse from the Bible? No. Because holy Qur'an has similar verses about Jews of that time,

Qur'an: O children of Israel! call to mind the (special) favour which I bestowed upon you, and that I preferred you to all others (for My Message). (2: 47and 122)

The issue is not about who is better or superior it is all about who follows and accepts the guidance of God. The above verses from the Qur'an and the Bible indicate that those who obey God are the chosen people. Jews consider themselves "the chosen people", Christians consider themselves "the saved people" and Muslims consider themselves to be "chosen" as well. All these claims do not say that the others are inferior. Whose claim is true will be determined by God, not by man.

Allah's (God's) Wrath for Non-Believers

Qur'an: They will do you no harm, barring a trifling annoyance; if they come out to fight you, they will show you their backs, and no help shall they get. Shame is pitched over them (like a tent) wherever they are found, except when under a covenant (of protection) from Allah, and from men; they draw on themselves wrath from Allah and pitched over them is (the tent of) destitution. This because they rejected the signs of Allah, and slew the prophets in defiance of right; this because they rebelled and transgressed beyond bounds. (3:111-12)

> *Qur'an:* Soon shall We cast terror into the hearts of the unbelievers, for that they joined partners with Allah, for which He had sent no authority: their abode will be the Fire; and evil is the home of the wrong-doers! (3:151)

The above verse seems to be a general statement about non-believers, but its application is very specific. The non-believers referred to here are, specifically, those people who had been terrorizing the State of Madinah for the past seven or eight years since the Muslims migrated from Makkah to Madinah. A reading of the verse in its true context shows that it cannot be interpreted as a general statement for all non-believers.

Now, let's read few verses from the Bible, and see what the Bible says about its non-believers.

> *Bible:* I will send my terror before you and will throw into confusion all the people against whom you shall come, and I will make all your enemies turn their backs to you. (Exodus, 23:27)

> *Bible:* Do not be yoked together with unbelievers. For what do righteousness and wickedness have in common? Or what fellowship can light have with darkness? (Corinthians, 6:14)

> *Bible:* What harmony is there between Christ and Belial? Or what does a believer have in common with an unbeliever? (Corinthians, 6:15)

But Muslims do not blame Jews and Christians or the Bible for spreading hate against non-Christians or non-Jewish. The above verses from the Qur'an and the Bible are condemning those opponents who were in conflict with the guidance of God during those times.

The following verse is sometimes exploited to support the idea that Jews are portrayed in a negative light in the Qur'an,

> *Qur'an:* Allah hath heard the taunt of those who say: "Truly, Allah is indigent and we are rich!", — We

shall certainly record their word and (their act) of slaying the Prophets in defiance of right, and We shall say: "Taste ye the penalty of the Scorching Fire!" (3:181)

First of all, there is no mention of Jews at all in this verse. However, if we assume it is about Jews, as many Muslim scholars have actually interpreted, the verse still cannot be generalized for all Jews. The people indicated in this verse were a specific people who lived fourteen centuries ago, and who mocked Muslims about giving charity. If anyone mocks Jewish scriptures today, don't we expect the Jews to have the right to respond to these taunts? Similarly, this verse is in specific response to those Jews who mocked the Qur'an fourteen centuries ago, and cannot be generalized towards all Jews.

Here are few verses from the Bible about such Jews and Christians.

> **Bible:** *Whoever closes his ear to the cry of the poor will himself call out and not be answered. (Proverbs, 21:13)*

> **Bible:** *But those who desire to be rich fall into temptation, into a snare, into many senseless and harmful desires that plunge people into ruin and destruction. (Timothy, 6:9)*

> **Bible:** *But if a righteous person stops doing good and starts doing all the evil, disgusting things that evil people do, will he go on living? No! None of the good he did will be remembered. He will die because of his unfaithfulness and his sins. (Ezekiel, 18:24)*

Is the Qur'an Anti-Semitic and Anti-Christian?

Let's review verses from Qur'an which are generally interpreted by Islamophobes and the terrorists anti-Semitic and anti-Christian.

> **Qur'an:** *"For the iniquity of the Jews We made unlawful for them certain (foods) good and wholesome*

---

which had been lawful for them; — in that they hindered many from Allah's way. — (4:160)

There is no anti-Semitism or anti-Christianism in this verse. It is about a specific people who lived during the time of the Prophet Moses (PBUH) who disobeyed him, and cannot be applied to all Jews. How about unlawful food mentioned in the Bible for Jews and Christians?

> **Bible:** *The LORD spoke again to Moses and to Aaron, saying to them, "Speak to the sons of Israel, saying, 'These are the creatures which you may eat from all the animals that are on the earth. Whatever divides a hoof, thus making split hoofs, and chews the cud, among the animals, that you may eat. Nevertheless, you are not to eat of these, among those which chew the cud, or among those which divide the hoof: the camel, for though it chews cud, it does not divide the hoof, it is unclean to you. Likewise, the shaphan, for though it chews cud, it does not divide the hoof, it is unclean to you; the rabbit also, for though it chews cud, it does not divide the hoof, it is unclean to you; and the pig, for though it divides the hoof, thus making a split hoof, it does not chew cud, it is unclean to you. You shall not eat of their flesh nor touch their carcasses; they are unclean to you.*

> *These you may eat, whatever is in the water: all that have fins and scales, those in the water, in the seas or in the rivers, you may eat. But whatever is in the seas and in the rivers that does not have fins and scales among all the teeming life of the water, and among all the living creatures that are in the water, they are detestable things to you, and they shall be abhorrent to you; you may not eat of their flesh, and their carcasses you shall detest. Whatever in the water does not have fins and scales is abhorrent to you. (Leviticus, 11: 1-12)*

> **Qur'an:** *For those who followed the Jewish Law, We forbade every (animal) with undivided hoof, and We*

*forbade them the fat of the ox and the sheep, except
what adheres to their backs or their entrails, or is
mixed up with a bone: this in recompense for their
willful disobedience: for We are True (in Our
ordinances). (6:146)*

This is not about all Jews. It is about those Jews who disobeyed
God's given laws and were guilty of insolence. They
disrespected their own Jewish laws. Similarly, a Muslim who
disobeys Allah will be guilty of insolence as well.

Bible: *Do not eat any detestable thing (Deuteronomy
14:3)*

Bible: *"Say to the Israelites: 'Do not eat any of the fat of
cattle, sheep or goats. (Leviticus 7:23)*

Bible: *Anyone who eats the fat of an animal from which
a food offering may be presented to the LORD must be
cut off from their people. And wherever you live, you
must not eat the blood of any bird or animal. Anyone
who eats blood must be cut off from their people.
(Leviticus 7:25, 26, 27)*

The following verse from the holy Qur'an is generally quoted on
almost every Islamophobe and terrorist websites.

Qur'an: *The punishment of those who wage war
against Allah and His Messenger, and strive with might
and main for mischief through the land is: execution,
or crucifixion or the cutting off of hands and feet from
opposite sides, or exile from the land: that is their
disgrace in this world, and a heavy punishment is
theirs in the Hereafter. — (5:33)*

Islamophobes quote such verses from the Qur'an to prove the
Qur'an spreads hatred towards Jews and Christians. These are
also among the verses terrorists use to prove that Muslims must
not be friendly to Jews and Christians. Both these groups are
dead wrong. Neither the Qur'an, nor our Prophet Muhammad
(PBUH) hates anyone, including Jews, Christians, pagans,

infidels, non-believers, atheists or agnostics. As in any religion, Islam may express disagreements with other religions and belief systems (and other religions and belief systems may express disagreement with Islam.) The right to this type of disagreement should be respected, and need not be automatically read as hate. Verse 5:33 from the Qur'an specifically addressed those individuals who were not only terrorizing the innocent people through violence, but also robbing trade caravans and individuals, and creating havoc in the society. They had murdered many innocent people, and the families of the victims were looking for justice. Finally, the terrorists were caught and brought to justice. Under no circumstances verse 5:33 was generalized and used against civilians and noncombatants of other religions.

What does the Bible say about the same kind of people?

> **Bible:** *And thou shalt consume all the people which the LORD thy God shall deliver thee; thine eye shall have no pity upon them: neither shalt thou serve their gods; for that will be a snare unto thee. (Deuteronomy, 17:16)*

> **Bible:** *eye for eye, tooth for tooth, hand for hand, foot for foot, burn for burn, wound for wound, stripe for stripe. (Exodus, 21:24-25)*

The Hypocrites

> **Qur'an:** *O Messenger! let not those grieve thee who race each other into Unbelief: (whether it be) among those who say: "We believe" with their lips but whose hearts have no faith; or it be among the Jews, — men who will listen to any lie, — will listen even to others who have never so much as come to thee. They change the words from their (right) times and places; they say "If ye are given this, take it, but if not, beware:" If anyone's trial is intended by Allah, thou hast no authority in the least for him against Allah. For such it is not Allah's will to purify their hearts. For them there is disgrace in this world, and in the Hereafter a heavy punishment. (5:41)*

This verse addresses a similar situation described in many parts of the Bible. When people deny and disobey the prophets of God, then God warns those people. There were a few deceitful people who tried to disguise themselves as Muslims, but in fact they were not Muslims. They tried to misguide and confuse newly converted Muslims. Those deceivers included pagans and a few Jewish people living in Madinah at that time, who pretended to be Muslim. Again, the verse should not be taken as a blanket condemnation of all Jews and all pagans.

> ***Qur'an:*** *The Jews say: "Allah's hand is tied up." Be their hands tied up and be they accursed for the (blasphemy) they utter. Nay both His hands are widely outstretched: He giveth and spendeth (of His bounty) as He pleaseth. But the revelation that cometh to thee from Allah increaseth in most of them their obstinate rebellion and blasphemy. Amongst them We have placed enmity and hatred till the Day of Judgment. Every time they kindle the fire of war, Allah doth extinguish it; but they (ever) strive to do mischief on earth. And Allah loveth not those who do mischief. (5:64)."*

This verse was revealed to the Prophet Muhammad (PBUH) in response to false accusations of some of the Jewish people living in Madinah. Once again, it is not about **all Jews**, but about those individuals trying to discourage the Muslims of that time from giving charity. The Qur'an refutes these attacks and defends the importance of charity in Islam. This is a normal and natural behavior – and certainly not a general statement against Jews.

How about the curses in the Bible?

> ***Bible:*** *I will bless those who bless you, and whoever curses you I will curse; and all peoples on earth will be blessed through you." (Genesis, 12:3)*

> ***Bible:*** *However, if you do not obey the Lord your God and do not carefully follow all his commands and decrees I am giving you today, all these curses will come on you and overtake you: (Deuteronomy, 28:15)*

Bible: He turned around, looked at them and called down a curse on them in the name of the Lord. Then two bears came out of the woods and mauled forty-two of the boys. (2 King, 2:24)

The recipients of these curses in the Bible were neither Jews nor Christians, but nonbelievers.

Qur'an: They do blaspheme who say: "Allah is Christ the son of Mary." But said Christ: "O children of Israel! worship Allah, my Lord, and your Lord." Whoever joins other gods with Allah—Allah will forbid him the Garden and the Fire will be his abode. There will for the wrong-doers be no one to help. (5:72)

Christians do not subscribe to Islam, just like Muslims do not subscribe to Christianity. So, for Christians, Muslims are unbelievers of Christianity and for Muslims, Christians are unbelievers of Islam. Is this not the reality? Muslims believe that the Son of Mary, Jesus Christ (PBUH) is a Prophet of God, while Christians see Jesus as either God, God incarnate, an aspect of God "made flesh", or the Son of God. This is the most fundamental difference between Christianity and Islam. Why should this difference in beliefs be seen as hate towards Christians, when it is only a disagreement on the role of Jesus Christ (PBUH)? This difference of opinion should be respected and should not be seen as hate towards Christians. Why do the Islamophobes not read the other verses of the holy Qur'an describing the honours of Jesus (PBUH). By name, Jesus is the most mentioned Prophet in the Qur'an. The miracles of Jesus Christ, his birth, his struggle and his message are repeatedly referred to in the holy Qur'an. There is an extensive chapter, Ale-Imran, on the ancestry of Jesus and a full chapter on his mother Mary (peace be upon her). The Qur'an is full of praises for Jesus and his mother Mary (peace be upon both of them)

Qur'an: But she [Mary] pointed to the babe (Jesus). They said: "How can we talk to one who is a child in the cradle?" He said: "I am indeed a servant of Allah: He hath given me revelation and made me a prophet; "And

He hath made me Blessed wheresoever I be, and hath enjoined on me Prayer and Charity as long as I live; "(He) hath made me kind to my mother, and not overbearing or miserable; "So Peace is on me the day I was born, the day that I die and the day that I shall be raised up to life (again)"! Such (was) Jesus the son of Mary: (it is) a statement of truth, about which they (vainly) dispute. (19: 29-34)

Qur'an: *"And Allah will teach him the Book and Wisdom, the Torah and the Gospel. "And (appoint him) a Messenger to the Children of Israel, (with this message): I have come to you with a sign from your Lord, in that I make for you out of clay as it were the figure of a bird, and breathe into it, and it becomes a bird by Allah's leave; and I heal those born blind, and the lepers and I quicken the dead by Allah's leave; and I declare to you what ye eat, and what ye store in your houses. Surely therein is a Sign for you if ye did believe. "(I have come to you), to attest the Law which was before me, and to make lawful to you part of what was (before) forbidden to you; I have come to you with a Sign from your Lord. So fear Allah and obey me. "It is Allah who is my Lord and your Lord; then worship Him. This is a way that is straight." (3:48-51)*

Qur'an: *Behold! The angels said: "O Mary! Allah hath chosen thee and purified thee; —chosen thee above the women of all nations. (3:42)*

Muslims love, respect and believe in Jesus Christ (PBUH).

Qur'an: *Strongest among men in enmity to the Believers wilt thou find the Jews and pagans; and nearest among them in love to the Believers wilt thou find those who say: "We are Christians:" because amongst these are men devoted to learning and men who have renounced the world, and they are not arrogant. (5:82)*

This verse addresses a specific situation that took place fourteen centuries ago. However, similar situations may arise again. In nations' lives, relationships with other nations do change under various circumstances. The above verse still reflects the reality of today's relationships between Christians and Muslims, and Jews and Muslims. The relationships between Christian and Muslims are relatively much more cordial than the relationships between Jews and Muslims. This is also a present reality of our times, whether we like it or not. However, I pray to almighty God to help in finding a resolution to the conflict between Israel and Palestine which will ultimately help in building better relationships between Jews and Muslims.

> **Qur'an:** *No just estimate of Allah do they make when they say: "Nothing doth Allah send down to man (by way of revelation)": Say: "Who then sent down the Book which Moses brought? — a light and guidance to man: but ye make it into (separate) sheets for show, while ye conceal much (of its contents): therein were ye taught that which ye knew not— neither ye nor your fathers." Say: "Allah (sent it down)": then leave them to plunge in vain discourse and trifling. (6:91)*

This is a response to those Jews in Madinah who refused to accept the Prophet Muhammad (PBUH) as the Messenger of God. They argued with Muslims about the validity of the Qur'an. The above verse was the response to them: if (you say) the Qur'an is not a book of God, then prove that the Torah is a book of God. Please note several Jewish residents of Madinah accepted Islam and became Muslim while some others remained Jewish.

> **Qur'an:** *Say: "O ye that stand on Judaism! if ye think that ye are friends to Allah, to the exclusion of (other) men, then express your desire for Death, if ye are truthful!" (62:6)*

This verse has a very specific context. In Madinah where Jews used to live they used to taunt the Muslims of Madinah with the concept that Jews were the chosen ones and dear to Allah. The Qur'an makes the point that if those Jews in Madinah were truthful in their claim that Allah loves them, then they should not consider death to be a bad thing. It is the death that moves a person from this world into the realm where he will be welcomed by God Himself. Once again, this verse is not against Jews. It was only an argument in a dialogue with the Jews of that time in Madinah.

> ***Qur'an:*** *Those who reject (Truth), among the People of the Book and among the Polytheists, will be in Hell-fire, to dwell therein (for aye). They are the worst of creatures. (98: 6)*

This verse describes the way Islam strongly distinguishes itself from other religions, just as other religions may describe how they distinguish themselves from Islam. But the intent of verse 98:6 is not, under any circumstances, to inspire Muslims to hate or discriminate against Jews, Christians or pagans.

> ***Bible:*** *But they mocked God's messengers, despised his words and scoffed at his prophets until the wrath of the Lord was aroused against his people and there was no remedy. (2 Chronicles, 36:16)*

> ***Bible:*** *Whoever believes in the Son has eternal life, but whoever rejects the Son will not see life, for God's wrath remains on them. (John, 3:36)*

Jihad (The Armed Struggle)

The root of the word "Jihad" is "Jahada" which means, "strive", "struggle", "persevere", "work hard to achieve certain objectives". For example, for the objective of spiritual growth, the holy Qur'an says:

> ***Qur'an:*** *And those who strive***("JAHAD")** *in Our (Cause) — We will certainly guide them to Our Paths: for verily Allah is with those who do right. (29: 69)*

Unfortunately, the word, "Jihad" has been abused and misused by Muslims themselves, to be taken up by Islamophobes everywhere, who now use "Jihad" in the same context as the terrorists – "The War" or "The Holy War". It is true that in the

---

holy Qur'an the word, Jihad has also been used for armed struggle, but the armed struggle of the Qur'an has a very different context from the one used by the terrorists and Islamophobes. The actual word used in the Qur'an for war is **Al-Harb.**

> *Qur'an: O ye who believe! fear Allah and give up what remains of your demand for usury, if ye are indeed believers. If ye do it not, take notice of war ("***HARB***") from Allah and His Messenger: but if ye repent ye shall have your capital sums; deal not unjustly and ye shall not be dealt with unjustly. (2:278, 270)*

Whenever the word "Jihad" is used for war in the holy Qur'an, it includes the entire struggle involved in the hardships of travel, sacrifice, loss of business and family time, donating money and resources, and only done for the purpose of securing the sovereignty of a country and bringing freedom to oppressed people. Does this not describe the practice in every country, including in the United States and all the Western world? Why is a Muslim country not allowed to defend its sovereignty in the same way a western country is? Struggling against the evil, and against the temptation to do wrong is Jihad. Standing up and speaking up or writing against a wrong in a society is also Jihad. Defending human rights is Jihad. Struggling for social justice is Jihad. Helping the needy and the oppressed is Jihad. Defending the sovereignty of the state is Jihad. Can this be wrong? Are these not western values as well?

The Islamic Laws for Armed Struggle (War)

1. According to Islamic principles, war cannot be legitimately declared by individuals or groups of individuals. A war can only be declared by an elected, legitimate government of a country. Organizations like Al Qaedah, Taliban, Daesh (ISIS), Al Nusrah, Boko Haram, Al Shabab, Lashkar Taiba, and Lashkar Jhangwi do not qualify as elected governments of any country; therefore, none of them has the right to declare or recruit for a war. Their behaviour cannot be called Jihad.

2. If a country is under attack or facing a threat of war from another country, then an elected, legitimate Islamic

---

government is required to defend the sovereignty of the country and can declare war (Jihad).

3. During armed struggle (Jihad) a Muslim army is required to follow the following laws.

   a. Children and women must not be killed even if they belong to enemy.

   b. Weapons of mass destruction which indiscriminately kill people are forbidden.

   c. Places of worship (all religions) must be protected.

   d. The Elderly, weak and sick cannot be killed.

   e. Green trees cannot be cut.

   f. Water sources (such as rivers, lakes and wells) cannot be contaminated even though they benefit the enemy.

   g. Prisoners of war must be treated humanely and must be provided sustenance.

   h. No one can be forced to convert to Islam.

These ethics or laws of war were given to Muslims by the Prophet Muhammad (PBUH) more than fourteen centuries ago – long before the Geneva Convention. Let us now examine a few more verses from the holy Qur'an, commonly exploited and misinterpreted by both terrorists and Islamophobes to justify their respective, malevolent agendas.

> **Qur'an:** *Fight in the cause of Allah those who fight you but do not transgress limits; for Allah loveth not transgressors. And slay them wherever ye catch them, and turn them out from where they have turned you out; for tumult and oppression are worse than slaughter; but fight them not at the Sacred Mosque, unless they (first) fight you there; but if they fight you slay them. Such is the reward of those who suppress faith. But if they cease, Allah is Oft-Forgiving Most Merciful. And fight them on until there is no more tumult or oppression and there prevail justice and faith in Allah; but if they cease let*

there be no hostility except to those who practise oppression. (2:190-193)

Based upon the above laws of Jihad (armed struggle), no verse on Jihad from the holy Qur'an can be used to cause harm to civilians, whether Muslim or non-Muslim. The verses cited only apply to a combat situation of two opposing armies facing each other on the battlefield, and specifically refer to the enemy combatants who were expected to attack Muslim pilgrims on their way to perform the Hajj. At the time the verses were revealed, Makkah was still under the control of pagans who had been brutally murdering Muslims for the past two decades. These pagans had already launched repeated attacks on Madinah city. They forced the Prophet Muhammad (PBUH), his family and his followers to leave Makkah – their ancestral homeland and birth place. When unarmed Muslims were going to perform the Hajj, they feared attacks from this same group of pagans. So, Allah commanded them to defend themselves *if they were attacked first.* Why do Islamophobes see hate in these verses? Don't they understand that people have the right to defend themselves against attack? Will the Canadian government not defend its citizens if anyone attacks them? Why does the government of a Muslim country not have the same right?

At the time of verses 2:190-193 were revealed, the pagans of Makkah assisted by other non-Muslim tribes and factions, had been attacking the city of Madinah for some time. Pagans had raged several wars against Muslims and made attempts to kill the Prophet Muhammad (PBUH). They had already killed many Muslims in numerous aggressive acts toward the city of Madinah that in modern language would answer to the term of **"terrorism"**.

In 628 Muslims from the city of Madinah went for the first time to perform the Hajj (pilgrimage) in Makkah with the Prophet Muhammad (PBUH). At that time Makkah was still a pagan city. One of the critical requirements of the Hajj is that the pilgrim must dress in a certain way called "ahraam" or "ihram", from some specific locations (called "meqat") around Makkah, and pronounce the intention of performing the Hajj. From meqat until Hajj is done a pilgrim cannot fight or even kill an insect. So when Muslims were planning to perform the Hajj, some of the Companions of the Prophet Muhammad (PBUH) raised the concerns about a potential attack by pagans. In ahraam, one cannot carry weapons which might be used to defend oneself against such an attack during the Hajj. This raised the possibility that the pilgrims might all be slaughtered by the pagans. What was to be done? The Companions asked the Prophet Muhammad (PBUH) for guidance in this matter. Allah responded with the above verse, telling Muslims to *defend themselves if and only if they were attacked by the pagans first.* As a final note here: since the pagans did not attack, no war or fighting took place at that time.

Does the Bible have similar verses? Answer: Yes.

> **Bible:** *"You must destroy all the peoples the LORD your God gives over to you. Do not look on them with pity and do not serve their gods, for that will be a snare to you." (Deuteronomy 7:16)*

> **Bible:** *"Moreover the LORD thy God will send the hornet among them, until they that are left, and hide themselves from thee, be destroyed." (Deuteronomy 7:20)*

> **Bible:** *"But the LORD thy God shall deliver them unto thee, and shall destroy them with a mighty destruction, until they be destroyed." (Deuteronomy 7:23)*

> **Bible:** *"And he shall deliver their kings into thine hand, and thou shalt destroy their name from under heaven: there shall no man be able to stand before thee, until thou have destroyed them." (Deuteronomy 7:24)*

> **Bible:** *The LORD is a man of war; the LORD is his name. (Exodus 15:2)*

> **Bible:** *eye for eye, tooth for tooth, hand for hand, foot for foot,*

> *burn for burn, wound for wound, stripe for stripe. (Exodus 21:24, 25)*

Bible: And, behold, one of them which were with Jesus stretched out his hand, and drew his sword, and struck a servant of the high priest's, and smote off his ear. (Matthew 26:51)

Bible: And they stoned Stephen, calling upon God, and saying, Lord Jesus, receive my spirit (Acts 7:59)

Bible: You shall chase your enemies, and they shall fall before you by the sword. Five of you shall chase a hundred, and a hundred of you shall chase ten thousand, and your enemies shall fall before you by the sword. (Leviticus, 26:7-8)

Bible: Your right hand, O LORD, glorious in power, your right hand, O LORD, shatters the enemy. (Exodus 15:6)

Are these Biblical verses not violent? Yet Muslims do not generally see them as being against non-believers of Jewish or non-Christian faiths. Why do Islamophobes take verses of the Qur'an out of context and misguide people?

More verses from the Qur'an on Jihad

Qur'an: Remember thy Lord inspired the angels (with the message): "I am with you: give firmness to the Believers: I will instill terror into the hearts of the Unbelievers: smite ye above their necks and smite all their finger-tips off them." (8:12)

Qur'an: And fight them on until there is no more tumult or oppression and there prevail justice and faith in Allah altogether and everywhere; but if they cease, verily Allah doth see all that they do. (8:39)

Qur'an: Against them make ready your strength to the utmost of your power, including steeds of war, to strike terror into (the hearts of) the enemies of Allah and your enemies and others besides whom ye may not know but whom Allah doth know. Whatever ye shall spend in the cause of Allah, shall be repaid unto you, and ye shall not be treated unjustly. (8:60)

The behaviour described in the above three verses from Surah Al-Anfal does not differ from what any army would do when their country is under attack. These Qur'anic verses are much softer and more lenient towards the combatants of an enemy army compared to what the United States and other Western countries' armies do to the combatants and civilians of their enemies. As with any country engaged in war, a Muslim country would also desire victory. Therefore, the verses in question are not about the supremacy of Islam, but about victory in a war. No army will engage itself in a war it does not want to win. Compare this to similar verses in the Bible.

> **Bible:** *And thou shalt consume all the people which the LORD thy God shall deliver thee; thine eye shall have no pity upon them: neither shalt thou serve their gods; for that will be a snare unto thee. (Deuteronomy, 7:16)*

> **Bible:** *Thou shalt not be affrighted at them: for the LORD thy God is among you, a mighty God and terrible. (Deuteronomy (7:21)*

> **Bible:** *And the LORD thy God will put out those nations before thee by little and little: thou mayest not consume them at once, lest the beasts of the field increase upon thee. (Deuteronomy (7:22)*

> **Bible:** *But the LORD thy God shall deliver them unto thee, and shall destroy them with a mighty destruction, until they be destroyed. (Deuteronomy 7:23)*

> **Bible:** *And he shall deliver their kings into thine hand, and thou shalt destroy their name from under heaven: there shall no man be able to stand before thee, until thou have destroyed them. (Deuteronomy, 7:24)*

> **Bible:** *When thou goest out to battle against thine enemies, and seest horses, and chariots, and a people more than thou, be not afraid of them: for the LORD thy God is with thee, which brought thee up out of the land of Egypt. (Deuteronomy, 20:1)*

Bible: For the LORD your God is he that goeth with you, to fight for you against your enemies, to save you. (Deuteronomy, 20:4)

Bible: And when the LORD thy God hath delivered it into thine hands, thou shalt smite every male thereof with the edge of the sword: (Deuteronomy, 20:13)

Bible: But the women, and the little ones, and the cattle, and all that is in the city, even all the spoil thereof, shalt thou take unto thyself; and thou shalt eat the spoil of thine enemies, which the LORD thy God hath given thee. (Deuteronomy, 20:14)

Bible: But thou shalt utterly destroy them; namely, the Hittites, and the Amorites, the Canaanites, and the Perizzites, the Hivites, and the Jebusites; as the LORD thy God hath commanded thee: (Deuteronomy (20:17)

Bible: Now go and smite Amalek, and utterly destroy all that they have, and spare them not; but slay man and woman, infant and suckling, ox and sheep, camel and ass. (Samuel, 15:3)

Having reviewed some Biblical verses referring to war, let us look at this Quranic verse intended for a similar situation.

Qur'an: Therefore, when ye meet the Unbelievers (in fight), smite at their necks; at length, when ye have thoroughly subdued them, bind a bond firmly (on them): therefore (is the time for) either generosity or ransom: until the war lays down its burdens. Thus (are ye commanded): but if it had been Allah's Will, he could certainly have exacted retribution from them (Himself); but (He lets you fight) in order to test you, some with others. But those who are slain in the way of Allah he will never let their deeds be lost. (47:4)

Again, the last (Quranic) verse is not for intended as instructions for behaviour in everyday life. Rather, it refers to combat missions, and entails very strict ethics for engaging enemy combatants in the battlefield. Under no circumstances should verse 47:4 or similar verses be taken as a guide for behaviour in non-combat situations.

9th Chapter (Surah Al Towbah)

This is probably the chapter of the holy Qur'an most often quoted and reviled by Islamophobes, who have often employed verses from this Surah to spread hate and fear against Islam and Muslims. These same Islamophobes often intentionally ignore the context of this entire Surah (chapter) and its verses.

> ***Qur'an:*** *But when the forbidden months are past, then fight and slay the pagans wherever ye find them, and seize them, beleaguer them, and lie in wait for them in every stratagem (of war); but if they repent, and establish regular prayers and practice regular charity, then open the way for them: for Allah is Oft-Forgiving, Most Merciful. (9:5)*

After Makkah, the birth place of Prophet Muhammad (PBUH), came under Muslim rule, Muslims were commanded to respect and fulfil all the agreements they had made with pagan tribes. After the victory in Makkah, Muslims did not do what generally a victorious army does – namely, go on a looting spree and become proud, arrogant, intimidating and violent. After the bloodless Muslim entry into, Makkah no one was ambushed and no one was forced to become Muslim. However, the verse was a precautionary guidance to Muslims that if someone attacks you, you do have the right to defend yourself and fight back. As a point of fact, no violence took place after Muslims got their victory. The few people were executed, were not punished in this way because they were non-Muslims, but because they had been fugitives, and hiding in Makkah. They had murdered innocent people, and their families were looking for justice. Here again, context may not be neglected.

Visiting the Holy Cities

> ***Qur'an:*** *O ye who believe! Truly the pagans are unclean; so let them not, after this year of theirs*

approach the Sacred Mosque. And if ye fear poverty, soon will Allah enrich you, if He wills out of His bounty for Allah is All-Knowing, All-Wise. (9:28)

In Islam, associating partners with God is known as "shirk" and is considered a contamination of beliefs. The Arabic word, "Najas" means "impure". The purity mentioned is one of beliefs, not of physical cleanliness. Here, "unclean" refers to the impurity of the beliefs of pagans who ascribed partners to God ("shirk"). The entire cities of Makkah and Madinah are Muslim sanctuaries. Due to very Islamic, sacred nature of these two cities, it is a requirement that no one enter these two cities with an impurity of beliefs. This restriction is made, not out of hate or discrimination for non-Muslims, but because of the sacred and extremely special nature of Makkah and Madinah. Consider this a visa entrance policy. Just as not everyone who applies for a visitor's visa to USA will be granted one, Islam holds a similar policy of entry criteria for Makkah and Madinah, and it is expected that people wanting to enter should meet these criteria. The two cities are not for sightseeing or partying. These two, entire cities are like sacred mosques for Muslim worship only. Otherwise, there are more than 52 other Muslim majority countries which also have Muslim holy sites, and anyone - Muslim or non-Muslim - can visit them without any restrictions.

Jizyah (Tribute)

> ***Qur'an:*** *Fight those who believe not in Allah nor the Last Day, nor hold that forbidden which hath been forbidden by Allah and His Messenger nor, acknowledge the Religion of Truth from among the People of the Book, until they pay the Jizyah with willing submission and feel themselves subdued. (9:29)*

This verse is not about war, but about the collection of taxes. Just as the IRS in the US and tax collecting agencies around the world are required to collect taxes, the treasury department of a Muslim State is also required to collect taxes from both its Muslim and non-Muslim citizens. The tax paid by Muslim citizens is called "zakat", and the tax paid by non-Muslim citizens is called "jizyah". The reason for identifying these two taxes separately, and managing or utilizing them separately, illustrates the extreme tolerance of Islam towards non-Muslims. The moneys collected as jizyah may not be used on the propagation of Islam, building mosques and benefitting the Muslim population. The jizyah money is to be used strictly for the security, safety and wellbeing of the non-Muslim population of the same area from where the jizyah money was collected. The word "subdued" is used here to refer to abiding by the laws of the land. Nothing more.

During the battle of Yarmouk, when the Muslim army had to make a strategic retreat, instructions were issued to return the jizya (tribute) to the people who had paid it. The reason for this was that the Muslim army was no longer able to provide security and care to the population of the area. Therefore, the money had to be returned.

> *Qur'an: The Jews call Uzayr (Ezra) a son of Allah and the Christians call Christ the son of Allah. That is a saying from their mouths; (in this) they but imitate what the Unbelievers of old used to say. Allah's curse be on them: how they are deluded away from the Truth! (9:30)*

This verse merely expresses the disagreement with Jews and Christians on the relationship of the Prophet Ezra (PBUH) and the Prophet Jesus (PBUH) with almighty God. Just as Jews and Christians disagree with some Islamic beliefs, Muslims also disagree with some Jewish and Christian beliefs. This disagreement should be a reason for dialogue, not a reason to hate each other. Muslims, Christians and Jews have more commonalities than differences.

> *Qur'an: They take their priests and their anchorites to be their lords in derogation of Allah, and (they take as their Lord) Christ the son of Mary; Yet they were commanded to worship but one Allah: there is no god but He. Praise and glory to him: (far is He) from having the partners they associate (with him). (9:31)*

Is this not true? Please read Jewish and Christian histories about how some of the Rabbis and Priests exploited Christians and Jews in the name of religion. Is this not still happening? Documentaries have been made and stories written on this very topic. This exploitation of people is not limited to Jews and Christians. A number of Muslim clergy and spiritual healers have also shown a willingness to exploit people in the name of religion. Unfortunately, people often follow them blindly. Such conditions can be found in every religion. This is one of the causes of extremism, corruption and violence. The Qur'an warns Muslims against placing blind, unthinking trust in their religious leaders.

> *Qur'an: O Prophet! strive hard against the Unbelievers and the Hypocrites, and be firm against them. Their abode is Hell— an evil refuge indeed. (9:73)*

In this verse Allah is guiding His Prophet (PBUH) to remain firm and strong against the unbelievers' and hypocrites' conspiracies and attempts to murder him. Allah is supporting and encouraging the Prophet Muhammad (PBUH) not to be discouraged by the opposition and animosity of the unbelievers and hypocrites of that time. There is nothing wrong with such guidance. Every commander guides his soldiers, every teacher encourages his/her students, and parents support and help their children during a time of difficult struggle. This verse, about the support and guidance of Allah for the Prophet Muhammad (PBUH), is not to be taken as against anyone.

> *Qur'an: Allah hath purchased of the Believers their persons and their goods; for theirs (in return) is the Garden (of Paradise): they fight in His cause, and slay and are slain: a promise binding on Him in Truth, through the Law, the Gospel and the Qur'an: and who is more faithful to his covenant than Allah? Then rejoice in the bargain which ye have concluded: that is the achievement supreme. (9:111)*

This verse, and other verses about armed struggle (war) are very specific for the Muslim army facing wars. They are not meant to instigate civilians to take up arms. Therefore, the civilians of the (original) Muslim State never acted as soldiers and fought against the enemy. If anyone wanted to join the army, then the person must join the army to be trained and to fight in the battlefield. This proves that the terrorism and violence against civilians is absolutely un-Islamic, unjust, criminal and punishable under Islamic law. Just as every army rewards and honours its soldiers due to their bravery and courage, Allah says the same: that the soldiers of a Muslim country will be honoured and rewarded with Heaven when they fight back and defend their country.

> *Qur'an: O ye who believe! Fight the Unbelievers who gird you about, and let them find firmness in you; and know that Allah is with those who fear him. (9:123)*

This does not represent a "carte blanche" for Muslims to go and "kill all the infidels" as many Islamophobes would have us believe. Muslims have never understood and acted on such verses in the manner the Islamophobes assert. The above, and similar verses are specific to conflict situations involving combat missions. And again, the combat missions must be declared by the government in authority and must be carried out in accordance with the Islamic rules of engagement described earlier. No private individuals or groups can declare Jihad.

Interfaith Dialogue

> *Qur'an: Say: "O people of the Book! come to common terms as between us and you: that we worship none but Allah; that we associate no partners with Him; that we erect not from among ourselves Lords and patrons other than Allah." If then they turn back, say: ye! "Bear witness that we (at least) are Muslims (bowing to Allah's will)." (3:64)*

The above verse of the holy Qur'an recognizes an important fact that among Jews, Christians and Muslims: that there is a common belief in one God between all three religions. Therefore, it is important for the leadership and the followers of these three Abrahamic religions to establish a dialogue to understand each other. The Prophet Abraham (Ibrahim) (PBUH), a common patriarch for all three religions, is described in the Qur'an as follows:

> *Qur'an: Abraham was not a Jew nor yet a Christian, but he was true in faith and bowed his will to Allah's and he joined not gods with Allah. (3:67)*

Muslims have lived in peace throughout the centuries with Christians and Jews. Islam recognizes Judaism and Christianity as religions and teaches Muslims to live in peace with the "people of the book" – the Jews and the Christians. Even with pagans, Islam coexists in peace.

> *Qur'an: Say: O ye that reject Faith! I worship not that which ye worship, Nor will ye worship that which I worship. And I will not worship that which ye have been wont to worship, Nor will ye worship that which I worship. To you be your Way, and to me mine. (Chapter 109, Surah Al-Kafirun)*

Women

Another piece of false propaganda, popular among Islamophobes, is that Islam treats women as second class citizens, and that women are not considered equal to men. Nothing could be further from the truth. Islamophobes try to justify this assertion with a few verses from Qur'an which supposedly "prove" their point. Ironically, the Islamophobic interpretation of these verses is identical to that of the extremists and the more rigid members of the Muslim clergy, who are a very small minority within the Muslim community. Let us discuss the verses in question.

> *Qur'an: Men are the protectors and maintainers of women, because Allah has given the one more (strength) than the other, and because they support them from their means. Therefore the righteous women are devoutly obedient, and guard in (the husband's) absence what Allah would have them guard. As to those women on*

whose part ye fear disloyalty and ill-conduct, admonish them (first), (next), refuse to share their, beds (and last) beat them (lightly); but if they return to obedience, seek not against them means (of annoyance): for Allah is Most High, Great (above you all). (4:34)

Another similar verse in the holy Qur'an,

Qur'an: *but men have a degree (of advantage) over them and Allah is Exalted in Power, Wise. (2:228)*

Apparently the above two verses from Qur'an do *seem* to endorse the idea of male superiority over female. But this is not true. In Islam there is no superiority based upon gender. In fact, Islam abolished all criteria of superiority based upon gender, skin colour, language, ancestry, lineage, wealth, status in the society, and any of the other pretexts used to place class people as "superior" or "inferior". The only criterion for superiority in Islam is righteousness.

Qur'an: *O mankind! We created you from a single (pair) of a male and a female, and made you into nations and tribes, that ye may know each other (not that ye may despise each other). <u>Verily the most honoured of you in the sight of Allah is (he who is) the most righteous of you.</u> And Allah has full knowledge and is well acquainted (with all things). (Surah Al Hujrat, 49:13)*

When we look at the life of the Prophet Muhammad (PBUH) he never behaved the way some reprobate Muslim men behave with their wives today. The Prophet Muhammad (PBUH) respected and loved his wives fully. He married several women, but none of them ever complained or ever mentioned any abuse - verbal or physical or of male domination in the family. The above verses do get misinterpreted by many Muslims and non-Muslims alike. However, the behaviour of Prophet Muhammad (PBUH) with his wives provides the correct understanding of these verses. They are not about the superiority of males, but define and describe roles and responsibilities in a family. The man (husband) has more responsibility over the woman. The man is responsible for making money, paying the mortgage, paying the bills, providing substance to the family and taking care of the family's needs. These verses are not about gender superiority but about the greater responsibility a man has in his family.

The Prophet Muhammad's (PBUH) first wife Hazrat Khadijah (May Allah's peace upon her) was the CEO of her business. The Prophet Muhammad's (PBUH) second wife Hazrat Aisha (May Allah's peace upon her) used to instruct the male Companions of the Prophet Muhammad (PBUH) after his death. Several women, including the Prophet Muhammad's (PBUH) own daughter, Hazrat Fatemah (May Allah's peace upon her) used to take care of wounded soldiers in the battlefield. There were hundreds of female scholars, leaders and entrepreneurs in the early history of Islam. Misogyny, domestic violence and discrimination against women is a major sin in Islam. It's a crime.

In his last sermon, the Prophet Muhammad (PBUH) said,

> *"O People it is true that you have certain rights with regard to your women, but they also have rights over you. Remember that you have taken them as your wives only under Allah's trust and with His permission. If they abide by your right, then to them belongs the right to be fed and clothed in kindness. Do treat your women well and be kind to them for they are your partners and committed helpers."*

> (delivered: 632 A.C. on the Ninth day of Dhul al Hijjah 10 A.H. in the 'Uranah valley of Mount Arafat.)

The relationship between husband and wife was described in such a beautiful way in the holy Qur'an fourteen centuries ago.

> *Qur'an: "They (wives) are your garments. And ye are their garments." (2:187).*

In Islam the salvation (Heaven) of everyone, man or woman, lies under the feet of a woman. That woman is your mother. The Prophet Muhammad (PBUH) made it compulsory for all men and women to be educated. During wars it is forbidden to kill women and children, even if they belong to the enemy. Honour killings and forceful marriages are not allowed in Islam and these are considered major crimes under the Islamic law. Details are discussed later in this book.

Let us review a few verses on women in the Bible.

> **Bible:** But the women, and the little ones, and the cattle, and all that is in the city, even all the spoil thereof, shalt thou take unto thyself; and thou shalt eat the spoil of thine enemies, which the LORD thy God hath given thee. (Deuteronomy, 20:14)

> **Bible:** And the children of Israel took all the women of Midian captives, and their little ones, and took the spoil of all their cattle, and all their flocks, and all their goods. (Numbers 31:9)

> **Bible:** And Moses said unto them, Have ye saved all the women alive? Behold, these caused the children of Israel, through the counsel of Balaam, to commit trespass against the LORD in the matter of Peor, and there was a plague among the congregation of the LORD. Now therefore kill every male among the little ones, and kill every woman that hath known man by lying with him. But all the women children, that have not known a man by lying with him, keep alive for yourselves. (Numbers, 31: 15-18)

> **Bible:** I do not permit a woman to teach or to assume authority over a man; she must be quiet. (Timothy, 2:12)

> **Bible:** women are to be silent in the churches. They are not permitted to speak, but must be in submission, as the Law says. (Corinthians 14:34)

Modest Dress (Hijab)

In Islam wearing modest dress is a requirement for men and women both.

Qur'an:O ye children of Adam! We have bestowed raiment upon you to cover your shame, as well as to be an adornment to you, But the raiment of righteousness,— that is the best. Such are among the signs of Allah, that they may receive admonition! (7:26)

For women one additional requirement of Qur'an is to cover their hairs just like in the Bible too.

Qur'an: Say to the believing men that they should lower their gaze and guard their modesty: that will make for greater purity for them: and Allah is well acquainted with all that they do. (30) And say to the believing women that they should lower their gaze and guard their modesty; that they should not display their beauty and ornaments except what (ordinarily) appear thereof; (24:30-31)

Bible: I also want the women to dress modestly, with decency and propriety, adorning themselves, not with elaborate hairstyles or gold or pearls or expensive clothes. (Timothy, 2:9)

Conclusion

In any country it is the government's responsibility to establish the rule of law. The verses from the Qur'an cannot be taken as blanket statements to force Islam on others. If this had been the case, then today Islam, with a present population of more than 23 per cent of the world's people, should have become the largest religion in the world. Muslims have ruled most of Eastern Europe and India for centuries; however, all these heavily populated countries are still have non-Muslim majorities. There is no hate or discrimination against non-Muslims in Islam. There is no superiority. There is no forcible conversion of non-Muslims to Islam. Citizens of a Muslim country do not expect the laws of their country to be enforced in all other countries.

It is huge misconception, and blatant hatemongering when Islamophobes insist that the Muslims in the Western countries are trying to replace the legal systems in these countries with the Sharia Law. This is an immense falsehood. In fact, Sharia Law itself dictates that a Muslim must obey and follow the laws of the country he or she lives in. Within the laws of Canada, a Muslim citizen of Canada has complete freedom to follow his/her religion. Religious freedom in Canada and in other Western countries clearly matches the requirements of Islam. Therefore, Islamophobes should stop misguiding Canadians and other citizens of western countries. Within the constitution of Canada or the United States or other western countries the religious freedom granted to citizens is the law that we all need respect and follow.

As far terrorists and their organizations are concerned, the overwhelming majority of Muslims, including all sects and denominations, unequivocally and unambiguously condemn them and do not consider them to be part of the 1.6 billion Muslims of the world.

Canadian Muslims love Canada, American Muslims love America, British Muslims love Britain, French Muslims love France and other Muslims, in turn, love their host countries. If a few Muslim youths are misguided by extremists, it does not follow that Islam and all Muslims should be held responsible for their crimes. We must build bridges among faith communities and establish peaceful civic dialogues among all faiths in order to have a better understanding of each other. The only way we can defeat extremism, terrorism, anti-Semitism, anti-Christianism, Islamophobia and anti-humanism is by acting in unity against hate, discrimination, racism, injustice, oppression and misguidance.

Among Jews, Muslims and Christians the unity and respect for each other is described by Allah in the Holy Qur'an.

Qur'an: *Not all of them are alike: of the People of the book are a portion that stand (for the right); they rehearse the signs of Allah all night long, and they prostrate themselves in adoration. They believe in Allah and the Last Day; they enjoin what is right, and forbid what is wrong; and they hasten (in emulation) in (all) good works; they are in the ranks of the righteous. Of the good that they do, nothing will be rejected of them; for Allah knoweth well those that do right. (3: 113-115)*

Part II

FATAWA (Islamic Edicts)

Due to the increasing influence of extremist and terrorist organizations on Muslim youth, Imam Syed B Soharwardy has formed a coalition with several Imams and Islamic scholars to issue formal religious edicts, called "Fatwa", on important issues and problems faced by the Muslims today. Issuing religious edicts, or Fatwa, are a very old process in Islam. It is used to provide guidance to ordinary Muslims on certain contentious questions, issues or problems. A Fatwa is a nonbinding religious edict by those Imams who are qualified in Islamic jurisprudence (Fiqh). So far, since 2009, the following Islamic edicts have been issued by the Islamic Supreme Council of Canada.

1. Fatwa on the Taliban and Al-Qaeda – May 12, 2009
2. Attacks on Canada and the United States are Attacks on Muslims, Too – January 8, 2010

3. Honour Killings, Domestic Violence and Misogyny Are Un-Islamic and Major Crimes – February 4,2012

4. Forced and Underage Marriages Are Un-Islamic – July 11, 2014

5. Historic Islamic Edict (Fatwa) on Joining Daesh (ISIS/ISIL) – March 11, 2015

6. Converts/Reverts, or potential converts to Islam, please take note. Your future is at stake – October 23, 2014

****

Date: May 12, 2009

Fatwa on Fighting Against the Taliban in Pakistan

At present, thousands of innocent Muslims in Pakistan are facing a very difficult time. They have become refugees in their own homeland due to the war between Pakistan's armed forces and extremists in the Swat valley. The United Nations has issued a public warning that the number of evacuees may soon exceed the one million mark. These innocent women, children elderly people and ordinary citizens are leaving their properties and livelihoods behind and facing a desperate situation. The current crisis was created by a group of self-righteous and self-appointed warlords and drug mafia disguised as clergymen. The government of Pakistan also bears a heavy degree of responsibility for initially helping the Taliban and allowing them to implement their way of life in the Swat valley under the disguise of "Islamic Shari'a". In reality, Islamic Shari'a and the Taliban's way of life are not the same thing. The Taliban's way of life is based upon ignorance, power hunger and hatred, and this is not acceptable to the overwhelming majority of Pakistani Muslims.

We support the actions of Pakistan's government in defeating the Taliban and urge all Pakistani Muslims to reject the Taliban's ideology. We hope that the Pakistani forces complete the current fight against the Taliban in order to eliminate any future possibility of "Talibanizing" the country of Pakistan. We request that the Canadian government provide disaster relief to the victims of the current crises in the Swat valley and financial assistance to Pakistan.

We also understand that the threat from the Taliban cannot be handled through a combat mission alone. The Taliban may be defeated by force, but "Talibanization" is an ideology that can only be defeated through education and economic stability. We request that the Canadian government help Pakistan in producing educational programs to create awareness about the un-Islamic and inhumane nature of the Taliban's ideology. Our scholars are ready to debate any Taliban leader on Islam and the current situation in Pakistan and Afghanistan.

It is every Pakistani's responsibility to help the victims of the Swat valley evacuation, and support all the efforts to counter the Talibanization of Pakistan. Talibanization is not Islam. Talibanization is a hateful ideology against the teachings of Qur'an and Prophet Muhammad (PBUH).

We must also make individual and collective du'a asking Allah to remove this affliction and bless us all. Ameen.

****

Date: January 8, 2010

An Attack on Canada and the United States is an Attack on Muslims, Too

In the Name of Allah, the Most Beneficent, the Most Merciful

We, the undersigned Imams, are issuing the following Fatwa in order to guide the Muslims of North America regarding the attacks on Canada and the United States by the terrorists and the extremists. In our view, these attacks are evil and Islam requires that Muslims stand up against this evil. In the holy Qur'an Almighty Allah orders Muslims,

"Let there among you be a group that summon to all that is beneficial commands what is proper and forbids what is improper; they are the ones who will prosper." (3:104)

"Believing men and believing women are protecting friends of one another; they enjoin what is right and forbid what is wrong; they perform salat and give zakat..." (9:71)

"Those who, if We establish them in the land (with authority), establish regular prayers and practice regular charity and enjoin the right and forbid the wrong..." (22:41)

Our beloved Prophet Muhammad (PBUH) said in a Hadith;

"When people see a wrong-doer and do nothing to stop him, they may well be visited by God with a punishment."

Therefore, it is an obligation upon us (Imams) to inform all Muslims around the world that Muslims in Canada and the United States have complete freedom to practice Islam. There is no single city in Canada and the United States where "masajid" (mosques) are not built. In all major cities, Islamic schools provide education to Muslim children about the Qur'an and the Islamic traditions. Thousands of Muslims perform Hajj every year and travel to Saudi Arabia with complete freedom and respect. In the month of Ramadan, both Canadian and the American governments recognize the occasion and greet all

Muslim citizens. Muslims pray five daily prayers in mosques without any fear or restrictions. Muslims have complete freedom to pay Zakat (alms) to the charity or a person of their choice. Muslims have complete freedom to celebrate their festivals openly, publicly and Islamically. Muslims enjoy freedom of religion just like Christians, Jews and others. No one stops us from obeying Allah and His Messenger (PBUH). No one stops us from preaching Islam and practicing Islam. In many cases, Muslims have more freedom to practice Islam here in Canada and the United States than in many Muslim countries.

In fact, the constitutions of the United States and Canada are very close to the Islamic guiding principles of human rights and freedom. There is no conflict between the Islamic values of freedom and justice and the Canadian or American values of freedom and justice.

Therefore, any attack on Canada and the United States is an attack on the freedom of Canadian and American Muslims. Any attack on Canada and the United States is an attack on thousands of mosques across North America. It is a duty of every Canadian and American Muslim to safeguard Canada and the USA. They must expose any person, Muslim OR non-Muslim, who would cause harm to fellow Canadians *or* Americans. We, Canadian and American Muslims, must condemn and stand up against these attacks on Canada and the United States.

May Allah save Canada, the United States and the entire world from the evil of wrong doers. Ameen.

Signed by 28 Canadian and the American Imams

****

Date: March 11, 2015

Historic Islamic Edict (Fatwa) on Joining Daesh (ISIS/ISIL)

All Praises are due to Alláh, we praise Him and we seek help from Him. We ask forgiveness from Him. We repent to Him; and we seek refuge in Him from our own evils and our own bad deeds. Anyone who is guided by Alláh, he/she is indeed guided; and anyone who has been led astray, will find no one to guide him/her. We bear witness that there is no god but Alláh, the Only One without any partner; and I bear witness that Muhammad (PBUH), is His servant, and His messenger. May Allah's peace and blessing upon you O' the messenger of Allah (PBUH).

FATWA (religious edict) on Joining ISIS/ISIL

We, the undersigned Imams, are issuing this Fatwa based upon the guidance of Allah in the holy Qur'an, the Sunnah of Prophet Muhammad (PBUH) and the consensus of the overwhelming majority of the scholars of Islam over the last fourteen centuries. We are issuing this Fatwa based upon the responsibility that Allah has prescribed in the holy Qur'an and in the Sunnah of Prophet Muhammad (PBUH).

Let there among you be a group that summon to all that is beneficial commands what is proper and forbids what is improper; they are the ones who will prosper. (3:104)

Believing men and believing women are protecting friends of one another; they enjoin what is right and forbid what is wrong; they perform salat and give zakat... (9:71)

Those who, if We establish them in the land (with authority), establish regular prayers and practice regular charity and enjoin the right and forbid the wrong... (22:41)

Our beloved Prophet Muhammad (PBUH) said in a Hadith:

When people see a wrongdoer and do nothing to stop him, God may well visit them with a punishment.

The holy Qur'an Allah has ordained that, without validation, a Muslim should not believe someone he/she is not sure of:

O ye who believe! If a wicked person comes to you with any news, ascertain the truth, lest ye harm people unwittingly, and afterwards become full of repentance for what ye have done. (49:6)

When the Hypocrites come to thee, they say, "We bear witness that thou art indeed the Messenger of Allah." Yea, Allah knoweth that thou art indeed His Messenger, and Allah beareth witness that the Hypocrites are indeed liars. (63:1)

Several other verses in the holy Qur'an, and several Hadith of the Prophet Muhammad (PBUH) clearly warn Muslims about the present and future presence of people apparently claiming to be Muslims, but who will, in fact, be imposters intent on deceiving Muslims in order to destroy them. Muslims must not trust such individuals or groups.

Prophet Muhammad (PBUH) said:

There will be dissension and division in my nation and a people will come with beautiful words but evil deeds. They recite the Qur'an but it will not pass beyond their throats. They will leave the religion as an arrow leaves its target and they will not return. They are the worst of the creation. (Sunan Abu Dawud, 4765)

Prophet Muhammad (PBUH) said:

In the last days, there will be young people with foolish dreams. They will say the best of words in creation but they will pass through Islam just as an arrow passes through its game. Their faith will not go beyond their throats. (Sahih Bukhari, 4770)

Who are ISIS/ISIL?

No Muslim ever heard the name of "Islamic State of Iraq and Syria (ISIS)" OR "Islamic State of Iraq and Levant (ISIL)" or

"Da'esh" (داعش), or the names of its leaders until few years ago. The sudden appearance of hitherto completely unknown persons, trying to take over the Muslim lands and the leadership of the Muslims in the Middle East, is very uncertain and suspicious. A few years ago, ISIS/ISIL was created by the funding of Western countries to overthrow the Syrian regime. These strangers cannot be trusted. Their claim to establish a "Caliphate" (Khilafah Al-Islamiyah) is very dubious, and cannot be trusted. The reasons are discussed later in this Fatwa.

O ye who believe! If a wicked person comes to you with any news, ascertain the truth, lest ye harm people unwittingly, and afterwards become full of repentance for what ye have done. (49:6)

During the first century of Islam a similar group emerged in Syria and Iraq. They were extremely violent people who murdered many members of the family and the companions of Prophet Muhammad (PBUH). The "Sahabah" and "Ahlul Bait" (the Companions and the Family of Prophet Muhammad (PBUH) identified and isolated that group and called them "the outsiders" (Khawarij). They did not accept them as a part of the Muslim community.

The strategy that the Khawarij used to destroy the Ummah is precisely the same as that being used today by the ISIS/ISIL and other terrorist organizations in current times. The Khawarij wanted to establish a "Caliphate" (Khilafah) based upon their own political agenda. Today, ISIS/ISIL is using the same word, "Caliphate (Khilafah)", to misguide and manipulate Muslims. ISIS and other terrorists are using the policies of the United States and other Western countries in the Middle East as an excuse to control Muslim sentiments and then utilize them for their own political and personal gain. In our opinion, these aforementioned terrorist organizations have been planted in Muslim countries to serve anti-Islam interests by deceiving Muslims in the name of Islam.

We, the undersigned Imams, strongly disagree and condemn those policies of the United States, Canada and other Western countries in the Middle East which are completely unjust, based upon Islamophobia, bias and intolerance towards Muslims. We also understand and condemn the highly destructive and hateful role of the media in intentionally promoting intolerance towards Islam and Muslims. However, in order to counter the anti-Islam and anti-Muslim efforts, a Muslim cannot choose the path of ISIS or other terrorist organizations like Al Qaeda, the Taliban, Boko Haram, Al-Shabab, Al-Nusrah, Lashkar Taiba, Lashkar Jhangwi, etc.

There is very clear guidance in the holy Qur'an and in the Sunnah of the Prophet Muhammad (PBUH) clearly guiding Muslims on how to handle anti-Islam and anti-Muslim aggression on the part of groups and governments. Under no circumstances does Islam allow the following. The following actions are un-Islamic and completely forbidden.

1. **Capturing opponents: Muslim OR non-Muslim civilians and beheading them.**

2. **Killing Muslims who disagree with the beliefs and actions of ISIS/ISIL.**

3. **Destroying mosques.**

4. **Demolishing the graves of Prophets (peace upon them), Aulia Allah (Saints) and ordinary people.**

5. **Forcing out Muslims or non-Muslims from their houses and making them refugees. There are now more than eight million refugees because of the atrocities of ISIS/ISIL.**

6. **Murdering Islamic scholars who oppose ISIS/ISIL.**

7. **Encouraging Muslim girls, and enabling them to travel secretly to Syria and Iraq to fight for an organization like ISIS/ISIL.**

8. **Burning enemy soldiers alive.**

9. **Mutilating a human body alive or dead.**

10. **Executing enemy combatants or civilians by throwing them from a height.**

ISIS/ISIL have committed all of the above violations in the most horrific and inhumane way. These actions are not allowed under any circumstances in Islam. Such actions are absolutely **"haraam"** (forbidden and a major sin) in Islam, and cannot be justified under any circumstances.

Nor can the struggle of ISIS/ISIL be considered "JIHAD". The clear guidance of Prophet Muhammad (PBUH) regarding armed struggle (war) is as follows.

1. During a war (Jihad), a Muslim army cannot do the following. These are the Jihad ethics of Islam that no one has the authority to change. These are also the Sharia laws about Jihad that no one can change.

    a. **Do not kill children, even if they belong to the enemy.**

    b. **Do not kill noncombatant men or women, even if they are from the ranks of the enemy.**

    c. **Do not kill elderly, sick or weak people, even if they are from the ranks of the enemy.**

    d. **Do not cut trees.**

    e. **Do not contaminate water.**

    f. **Do not destroy the places of worship of any religion.**

    g. **Do not force people against their will to convert to Islam.**

2. War (Jihad) cannot be declared by individuals or groups of people. Only an Islamic government with its authority on a state can declare war (Jihad) if the state is being attacked. (Note: ISIS/ISIL was not a government of any state. They were created by western interests in the region to benefit western interests by removing the Syrian government).

ISIS/ISIL has violated all of the above prohibitions of Islam. They have disobeyed the Qur'an and the guidance of Prophet Muhammad (PBUH) therefore, their struggle cannot be an Islamic struggle and their war cannot be called "Jihad". Rather, it is pure terrorism and haraam. The behavior and the actions of ISIS/ISIL has consistently proven that they are NOT Muslims and they cannot be trusted by the Muslims.

Anas ibn Malik (May Allah be pleased with him) reported:

The Messenger of Allah, peace and blessings be upon him, said, "There will be dissension and division in my nation and a people will come with beautiful words but evil deeds. They recite the Qur'an but it will not pass beyond their throats. They will leave the religion as an arrow leaves its target and they will not return until the arrow returns to its notch. They are the worst of the creation. Blessed are those who fight them and are killed by them. They call to the Book of Allah but they have nothing to do with it. Whoever fights them is better to Allah than them." (Sunan Abu Dawud 4765).

Famous scholar of Islam Imam Ibn Kathir writes:

"If the Khawarij ever gained power, they would corrupt the entire earth, Iraq, and Syria. They would not leave a boy or a girl or a man or a woman, for in their view the people have become so corrupt that they cannot be reformed except by mass killing." (Al-Bidayah wa Nihayah 10/584)

We warn all Muslims, especially the youth, regarding the very deceptive un-Islamic, criminal nature of ISIS / ISIL OR Da'esh (داعش). This organization has recruited several Muslim youth, girls and boys, by deceiving them in the name of the Khilafah (Caliphate). Some Muslim youth from Western and Islamic countries have been misguided by ISIS/ISIL (Da'esh). We urge all of them to repent to Allah and leave ISIS/ISIL immediately.

We, the undersigned Imams inform all Muslim youth, girls, boys and general public that:

- Joining ISIS/ISIL and groups like ISIS/ISIL is *haraam* (forbidden) in Islam.

- Any Muslim who joins these Khawarij (ISIS/ISIL) groups actually disconnects and disassociates himself/herself from the Ummah of Prophet Muhammad (PBUH).

- Any Muslim who joins ISIS/ISIL OR similar groups disobeys Allah and His Prophet Muhammad (PBUH).

And whosoever disobeys Allah and His Messenger (PBUH), and transgresses His limits, He will cast him into the Fire, to abide therein; and he shall have a disgraceful torment. (4:14)

- Any Muslim who helps, facilitates travel, provides funds for, or encourages a Muslim to join ISIS/ISIL and groups like ISIS/ISIL commits *"haraam"* (a sinful action that is forbidden to be done). Such a person will not only be punished by Allah for misguiding Muslims, but will also be responsible for the crimes committed by the people he/she has motivated.

- Any Muslim who helps, directly or indirectly, any organization, agency, group, individual or government which supports facilitates or motivates Muslim girls or boys to travel secretly **or** without the consent of parents to join ISIS/ISIL or any other terrorist organization, commits haraam and will face the wrath of Allah in this world and in the next world. (No Muslim parents will ever give consent to join ISIS/ISIL knowing the un-Islamic nature of ISIS.)

Ye are the best of peoples, evolved for mankind, enjoining what is right, forbidding what is wrong, and believing in Allah. (3:110)

We strongly urge every Muslim, especially the youth, not to be influenced by the speeches, songs and the literature available on the Internet or on social media produced by the imposters pretending to be Muslims. This is a trap for young Muslims. They must visit their local mosques and discuss any questions or points of confusion with the Imam publicly. Any person who inspires people to cause harm to Canada and Canadians must immediately be reported to the Police. This is our Islamic duty, as Canada is a country where more than 1.1 million Muslims live, more than 1000 mosques have been built in every part of the country, more than 700 Islamic schools (madrasah) are educating Muslim children and adults, where large gatherings on Islam, Qur'an and Prophet Muhammad (PBUH) are freely and publicly held, and where every day several non-Muslim Canadians embrace Islam. Muslims have complete freedom to practice Islam in Canada.

Therefore, any attack on Canada will be an attack on the freedom of Canadian Muslims. It is the duty of every Canadian Muslim to safeguard Canada. May Allah save Canada and the entire world from the evil ISIS/ISIL and other of wrong doers. Ameen.

O ye who believe! Obey Allah and His Messenger, and turn not away from him when ye hear (him speak). (20) Nor be like those who say "we hear", but listen not: (8:21)

We pray for peace and justice for every human on this planet. And on us is nothing but to convey/deliver.

Thank you.

Signed by 38 Canadian Imams and Islamic leaders

****

Date: February 4, 2012

Honour Killings, Domestic Violence and Misogyny Are Un-Islamic and Major Crimes

(Mississauga) On the blessed day of Eid Milad un Nabi (the birthday of Prophet Muhammad, PBUH), the thirty-four Imams and the Islamic leaders affiliated with the Islamic Supreme Council of Canada have issued the following Fatwa reminding Muslims that honour killings, domestic violence and misogyny are un-Islamic actions and crimes in Islam. These crimes are major sins in Islam punishable by the court of law and almighty Allah.

FATWA (religious edict)

In the Name of Allah, the Most Beneficent, the Most Merciful

We, the undersigned Imams, are issuing this Fatwa as a reminder to the Muslims of North America regarding the issues of domestic violence, honour killings and misogyny in our society. The recent Shafia family trial in Kingston, Ontario has reminded all of us that we need to do more in order to prevent such tragedies in the future. There are some Muslims who would commit a crime and then use Islam to justify their crime. According to the Qur'an the biggest liar is the one who tells lies on Allah.

There is no justification for honour killings, domestic violence and misogyny in Islam. These are crimes in the court of law and in the sight of Allah. Therefore, this Fatwa is issued based upon the command of almighty Allah in the holy Qur'an;

"Let there among you be a group that summon to all that is beneficial commands what is proper and forbids what is improper; they are the ones who will prosper." (3:104)

"Believing men and believing women are protecting friends of one another; they enjoin what is right and forbid what is wrong; they perform salat and give zakat..." (9:71)

"Those who, if We establish them in the land (with authority), establish regular prayers and practice regular charity and enjoin the right and forbid the wrong..." (22:41)

Our beloved Prophet Muhammad (PBUH) said in a Hadith;

"When people see a wrong-doer and do nothing to stop him, they may well be visited by God with a punishment."

It is an obligation upon us (the Imams) to inform all Muslims in Canada and around the world that in Islam:

1. Honour killings, domestic violence, misogyny, spousal abuse, child abuse in all forms are forbidden.

2. The relationship between the husband and wife is based upon mutual love and kindness.

"And among His Signs is this, that He created for you mates from among yourselves, that ye may dwell in tranquility with them, and He has put love and mercy between your (hearts): verily in that are Signs for those who reflect." (30: 21)

In the event of a family dispute, the Qur'an urges husbands to treat their wives with kindness.

"Live with them on a footing of kindness and equity. If ye take a dislike to them it may be that ye dislike a thing, and Allah brings about through it a great deal of good." (4: 19)

"And in no wise covet those things in which Allah hath bestowed His gifts more freely on some of you than on others: to men is allotted what they earn, and to women what they earn: but ask Allah of His bounty: for Allah hath full knowledge of all things." (4:32)

In Islam there is no gender based superiority. In fact, the relationship between a husband and wife is based upon mutual love, respect and care.

"They (wives) are your garments. And ye are their garments." (2:187)

3. Some people quote the following verse from the holy Qur'an to prove that a man has superiority over his wife.

".... but men have a degree over them (wives) and Allah is Exalted in Power, Wise." (2:228)

The above verse is not about the superiority of the man. Rather, it is about the greater responsibility of the man in running the home such as fulfilling the food, shelter, clothing, education and safety needs of family members.

The Qur'an recognizes gender equality. The idea of superiority is based on honesty and piety only.

"O Mankind, We created you from a single (pair) of a male and a female and made you into nations and tribes, that you may know each other. Verily the most honored of you in the sight of Allah is he who is the most righteous of you" (49:13).

4. We would also like to clarify the translation of verse 34 of Surah Al Nisa. Some translators have the Arabic word, "wadhriboo-hunnah" (وَٱضْرِبُوهُنَّ) translated as "strike" OR "hit" (with toothbrush). In our opinion, this is not the correct translation.

In a case when a married woman develops a sexual relationship outside the marriage, the Qur'an requires the husband to follow three steps and not to become violent.

a. First educate her

b. Second take separate beds

c. Report (cite) her to a (religious) authority (appoint an arbitrator)

Here is the correct translation of verse 4:34.

The men are supporters/maintainers of the women with what God bestowed on some of them over others and with what they spent of their money, so the righteous women are dutiful; guardians to the unseen with what God guarded. And as for those women you fear their disloyalty, then: (first) you shall advise them, and (second) abandon them in the bed, and (lastly) *cite* **them (to the authority). If they obeyed you, then seek not against them a way; Truly, God is High, Great. [4:34]**

5. In Islam, the obedience of Allah is NOT acceptable to Allah unless the person does it with his or her heart. In Islam, the reward of a good deed from Allah depends on a person's intention. If the person is forced to do certain things against his/her will then there is no reward from Allah.

"There is no compulsion in religion." (2:256)

Therefore, beating or abusing a family member in order to force that person to follow Islam is not acceptable to Allah. Parents have the responsibility to educate children about the teachings of Islam but they have no right to abuse or harm them. They need to be role models for their own children. The Prophet Muhammad (PBUH) said, "Help the oppressed and the oppressor". People asked the Prophet Muhammad (PBUH): "We understand how to help the oppressed, but how should we help the oppressor?" He replied, "By stopping him from committing acts of oppression".

In Islam, if a person commits un-Islamic actions (crimes) an institution with authority, such as the police, courts or government, can punish that person – not family members or other private citizens. Honour killing is a major sin in Islam. Those who commit honour killings should face the justice of this world, and they will face Allah's justice as well.

Those who cause harm to a family member, or anyone else, because they believe that family member, or that person, has brought disgrace to them - or that their honour has been damaged by his or her actions - commit both a major sin and a crime by taking the law into their own hands. Only the court system of a country has the authority to determine guilt or innocence, and to punish a person, not the person's family members, such as the father, mother, husband, brother, etc.

Honour killing is an un-Islamic practice which has roots in paganism. In Islam, killing or hurting someone in the name of honour is a criminal act which should be punished by a court of law, and it will be punished by Allah on the judgement day.

6. Domestic violence is a huge problem across the world. We believe it is not a Muslim problem. It is a human problem. Domestic violence crosses all boundaries. Domestic violence exists in the developed and in the developing worlds. Domestic violence takes place in houses of all persuasions, including Christian, Jewish, Muslim, Buddhist, Hindu, Atheist, and Agnostic houses. It is everywhere. However, as Muslims we must follow the holy Qur'an and the teachings of the Prophet Muhammad (PBUH) which forbids causing harm to children, wives or any other person due to disagreements, disputes or conflicts. All family issues must be resolved according to the laws of the country we live in.

As the Imams and religious leaders in the community, we have an obligation to inform everyone that Islam condemns domestic violence, honour killings and misogyny. We offer every Muslim family in Canada and the United States the support and guidance they need if a family member seems to be violating the Islamic code of conduct. However, we want to be very clear that no one, except the Canadian or American courts, has the right to punish anyone. It is the requirement of Islam that citizens must follow and respect the laws of their countries. Therefore, Muslims who live in Canada must follow and respect the laws of Canada. Similarly, American Muslims must follow the laws of the United States.

On this important day of Eid Milad un Nabi (PBUH), the Islamic Supreme Council of Canada announces **"ISCC Families Network"** project, which will be rolled out across North

America in cities where ISCC's affiliated mosques and organizations exist. This network will work with the young girls and the boys and their parents to help and guide them in resolving issues and conflicts. The network will establish separate girls' and boys' clubs where these young people can discuss issues, and share their experiences at home, at school and at work. This network will establish working relationships with the police, teachers and other mainstream Canadian and the American organizations in the field of domestic violence, racism, discrimination and bullying. All the services provided by this network will be free to all families.

We pray for the victims of domestic violence and honour killings especially the victims of Shafia family. We extend our full support to the victims of domestic violence. We request all the Canadian and the American Muslims to join "ISCC Families Network". May Allah guide us and protect all of us from the evil of Satan and the wrongdoers. Ameen.

Signed by 34 Imams and Islamic scholars:

****

Date: July 11, 2014

Forced and Underage Marriages Are Un-Islamic

(Calgary) During the blessed days of Ramadan, the thirty-five Imams and the Islamic leaders affiliated with the Islamic Supreme Council of Canada have issued the following Fatwa reminding Muslims that forced marriages and marriages with underage girls are un-Islamic actions and crimes in Islam. These crimes are major sins in Islam punishable by the court of law and the Almighty Allah.

FATWA (Religious Edict)

In the Name of Allah, the Most Beneficent, the Most Merciful

We, the undersigned Imams, are issuing this Fatwa as a reminder to the Muslims of North America regarding the issues of forced marriages and the marriages of underage girls and boys.

We know very well that there are a few parents who believe they can force their daughters to marry only men of the parents' choosing, and there are a few Muslims who believe marrying underage girls is permissible. However, based upon the guidance in the holy Qur'an and the teachings of Prophet Muhammad (PBUH), these are very un-Islamic, criminal actions. Such marriages are forbidden (haraam) in Islam.

According to the holy Qur'an, the biggest liar is the one who tells lies on Allah. There is no justification for such practices in Islam. These are crimes in the court of law and in the sight of Allah. Therefore, this Fatwa is issued, based upon the command of Almighty Allah in the holy Qur'an:

- **"Let there among you be a group that summon to all that is beneficial commands what is proper and forbids what is improper; they are the ones who will prosper." (3:104)**

- "Believing men and believing women are protecting friends of one another; they enjoin what is right and forbid what is wrong; they perform salat and give zakat…" (9:71)

- "Those who, if We establish them in the land (with authority), establish regular prayers and practice regular charity and enjoin the right and forbid the wrong…" (22:41)

Our beloved Prophet Muhammad (PBUH) said in a Hadith:

- "When people see a wrong-doer and do nothing to stop him, they may well be visited by God with a punishment."

It is an obligation upon us (the Imams) to inform all Muslims in Canada and around the world that in Islam:

1. Forced marriage is not recognized as lawful marriage. The relationship between the husband and wife is based upon mutual love and acceptance.

2. Marrying an underage girl is cruel and criminal.

- "And among His Signs is this, that He created for you mates from among yourselves, that ye may dwell in tranquility with them, and He has put love and mercy between your (hearts): verily in that are Signs for those who reflect." (Qur'an, 30: 21)

- "Ye who believe! Ye are forbidden to inherit women against their will. Nor should ye treat them with harshness…" (Qur'an, 4:19)

- "They (wives) are your garments. And ye are their garments." (2:187)

The Holy Prophet Muhammad (PBUH) has emphatically forbidden forced marriages. He has unequivocally stated that in order for a marriage to be Halaal (legal/permissible), the guardian or parents must ask permission from the female to be taken in marriage. A marriage cannot go ahead unless the woman is consulted and she has given her approval for the marriage. If she refuses, and does not want to get married, then her wish must be respected and others may not go against her decision.

The Prophet Muhammad (PBUH) said:

- **"A matron should not be given in marriage until she is consulted, and a virgin should not be given in marriage until her permission is sought."** (Tirmidhi, Book 11, Vol. 2, Book 6, Hadith 1107)

- **"A matron should not be given in marriage except after her permission; and a virgin should not be given in marriage except after her permission. "(Bukhari, Book 62, Vol 7, Hadith 67)**

- *Abu Hurairah (May Allah be pleased with him) said:* **"The Messenger of Allah (PBUH) said:** *'An orphan girl should be consulted with regard to marriage, and if she remains silent, that is her permission. If she refuses then she is not to be forced.'"* **(Nasa'I, Book 26, Vol. 4, Book 26, Hadith 75 and Tirmidhi, Book 11, Hadith 30. Vol. 2, Book 6)**

- **Narrated by Abdullah ibn Abbas (May Allah be pleased with him): "A girl came to the Prophet (PBUH) and mentioned that her father had married her against her will, so the Prophet (PBUH) allowed her to exercise her choice." (Abi Dawud, Book 12, Hadith 51)**

Thus, it is clear from the several sayings of the Prophet Muhammad (PBUH) that parents cannot force a daughter to marry a man whom she does not approve of. For a marriage to be valid in Islam there has to be mutual consent, from both the bride and the groom.

Marriage is one of the most important institutions of Islam. The Prophet Muhammad (PBUH) declared that when a person marries he has completed "half of his religious obligations." **Marriage is a legal contract between two individuals. It requires the usual mutual consent between the parties**, specified conditions, and a public witness. The involvement of parents and family extends only to help in finding the right partner. For a successful, long lasting marriage, it is essential to consider long-term compatibility, moral character and religious beliefs. However, an arranged marriage may not be a forced marriage and Islamic law stipulates that the free consent of both parties is necessary for its validity.

Evidence in the Quran and the sayings of the Prophet Muhammad (PBUH) clearly shows that forced marriages are not a part of Islam. It is apparent that forcing a marriage upon someone against that person's will is forbidden in Islam.

The above-mentioned Ahadith (sayings) of Prophet Muhammad (PBUH) make it obvious that the girl to be married must first reach an age when she has developed all the cognitive faculties necessary to analyse the pros and cons of her prospective marriage. She must be mature enough to make a conscious decision about her future life and to select her spouse. An underage girl (or, for that matter, a boy) is not mature enough to make such a rational and intelligent decision, which will have life-impacting effects. Therefore, it is a clear violation of the teachings of the Prophet Muhammad (PBUH) to marry an underage girl. Once again, parents cannot make a decision or choose a spouse for their daughters. They can only facilitate, guide and advise their children, girls or boys.

Some people try to use the following verse of the holy Qur'an as an excuse to justify underage marriages:

> • **"And if you are in doubt about those of your women who have despaired of menstruation, (you should know that) their waiting period is three months, and the same applies to those who have not menstruated as yet. As for pregnant women, their**

period ends when they have delivered their burden. "(Qur'an, 65:4)

Those who justify underage marriages say that the section in the above verse, "...those who have not menstruated yet," refers to underage girls. This is a complete misinterpretation of the Quran. The Quran is not referring to underage girls here, but to women who have stopped menstruating for some medical reason (which is not uncommon).

Some people use a Hadith quoted in Bukhari regarding the age of Hazrat Aisha Siddiqah (May Allah be pleased with her) when she married Prophet Muhammad (PBUH). According to this Hadith when Hazrat Aisha (May Allah be pleased with her) married the Prophet Muhammad (PBUH) she was 9 years old.

All the scholars of Islam are unanimous in understanding that the holy Qur'an supersedes every other writing, including Hadith. Moreover, there are several categories of Hadith, and every Hadith in the books of Hadith is not necessarily authentic *OR* correct. This particular Hadith has been disputed by several scholars and is considered a misquoted or "fabricated Hadith". Reasons for doubting the authenticity of this Hadith include the evidence that it clearly conflicts with the character of the holy Prophet (PBUH) as described in the holy Qur'an.

The character of the Prophet Muhammad (PBUH) described in the holy Qur'an is:

- **"And thou (standest) on an exalted standard of character." (Qur'an, 68:4).**

- **"Ye have indeed in the Messenger of Allah a beautiful pattern (of conduct)..." (Qur'an, 33:21)**

It would be immoral for a person in his late fifties to marry a girl of only 9 years of age. Our Prophet Muhammad (PBUH) is on the top of morality. This world had never seen and will never see anyone more moral and spiritual than the last Messenger of Allah, Muhammad (PBUH). Therefore, it is a lie and a piece of false information that Hazrat Aisha (May Allah be pleased with her) married Prophet Muhammad (PBUH) when she was underage. A wealth of evidence suggests that she was no less than nineteen (19) years when she was married to the Prophet Muhammad (PBUH). For a detailed analysis and evidence regarding the age of Hazrat Aisha (May Allah be pleased with her) when she married, please refer to the following website address:

http://islamicsupremecouncilofcanada.com/ummul-momineen-hazrat-ayesha-may-allah-be-pleased-with-her/

The Prophet Muhammad (PBUH) gave no recognition to class distinction. On the contrary, in marriage, he emphasized compatibility. When a man questioned the Prophet of Islam (PBUH) about whom he should marry. The Prophet replied, *"Your match,"* One of the most prominent jurists of Islam, Imam Ja'far Al Sadiq (May Allah be pleased with him) said, *"An intelligent and wise woman must not be matched except with a sage and wise man."*

"There is no compulsion in religion…" (Qur'an, 2:256)

As Imams and religious leaders in the community, we have an obligation to inform everyone that Islam forbids forced and/or underage marriages. We offer every Muslim family in Canada and the United States the support and guidance they need if a family member seems to be violating the Islamic code of conduct. However, we want to be very clear that no one, except the Canadian or American court, has the right to punish a crime. Islam requires that citizens must follow and respect the laws of their countries. Therefore, Muslims who live in Canada must follow and respect the laws of Canada. Similarly, American Muslims must follow the laws of the United States.

Signed by 36 Imams and Islamic scholars

Article

Converts/Reverts, or potential converts to Islam, please take note. Your future is at stake.

Introduction

Due to the divisions among Muslims, it can be very confusing for many western people who want to convert/revert to Islam to know which version of Islam is the true Islam. Moreover, the recent escalation in the radicalization of Muslim converts and their exploitation by extremist groups is alarming and dangerous. Therefore, it is important to understand what Islam is and what is NOT Islam. In this article I am not going to discuss why someone would convert to Islam? I am assuming that (hypothetical) person has acquired some basic understanding of Islam and now is willing to become a Muslim.

When a person wants to convert/revert to Islam he/she must consider the following two most important criteria for deciding which Imam or group can guide this individual towards the true Islam.

1. What interpretation of the Qur'an and Sunnah has been followed by the greatest majority of Muslim scholars throughout the fourteen centuries of Islam? Does this Imam or group follow the same interpretation, or do they follow something different?

2. What traditions of Islam have been followed by the overwhelming majority of Muslims throughout the fourteen centuries of Islam? Does this Imam or group follow the same traditions or do they advocate something completely different?

Background and Confusion

Starting from the first century of Islam, Muslims were divided into two denominations. A Small minority separated themselves from the majority and between 10% to 15% of these Muslims identified themselves as "Shia" while the rest of the Muslims identified themselves as "Sunni" (Ahle Sunnah wal Jama'h). I am not going to discuss the reasons for this division. Moreover, the Shia-Sunni divide has not been known to create a major confusion for potential converts. The major source of confusion and/or misguidance for many converts is the existence of several groups (sects) within Sunni denomination. Therefore, I shall discuss the historical Sunni understanding and interpretation of Islam. Over the years quite a few sects or groups have emerged from the Sunni denomination – each one identifying itself as, "Sunni Muslim" – but mostly embracing interpretations of the Qur'an and Sunnah that the majority of Sunni scholars have never accepted.

The First Deviants

During the first century of Islam a faction emerged from the region now identified as Syria and Iraq. The followers of this group claimed they understood the Qur'an and Sunnah better than the thousands of Companions of Prophet Muhammad (PBUH). This group refused to accept the authority of the government. They refused to follow the laws of the country and created rebellion against the third Caliph of Islam Hazrat Osman Ibn Affan (May Allah be pleased with him). They murdered him. When the fourth Caliph Hazrat Imam Ali Ibn Abi Talib (Allah be pleased with him), who was also the cousin and the son-in-law of Prophet Muhammad (PBUH), took over power they refused to accept him as the ruler, and murdered him as well! This group had a very strange interpretation of Qur'an. Their interpretation was completely new and far removed from the understanding of thousands of Muslims who had accepted Islam right in front of the Prophet Muhammad (PBUH). This latter group, known as "the companions" (Sahabah) had learnt the Qur'an and Islam directly from the Prophet Muhammad (PBUH); however, the followers of the breakaway group refused to accept the interpretation of the Sahabah and murdered thousands of the companions. This deviant group were extremist, very violent people. Although they were a small minority, their terrorism was massive and caused irreparable damage to Muslims. In history they are recognized as *"Khawarij"* (outsiders of Islam). The vast majority of Muslims have NEVER agreed with the *Khawarij* interpretation of the Qur'an and Sunnah. With the passing of time, the Khawarij group diminished and slowly ended.

The Division

Although the Khawarij were isolated, and finally became extinct, Muslims have remained divided into Sunni and Shia schools of thoughts. Over the several centuries, the Shia denomination became further divided into several groups, such as: Ismaili, Ithna Ashari, Bohra, and Alavi. The followers of these Shia sects have identified themselves, accordingly, with their sects, for example: Ismaili Shia Muslims, Ithani Ashri Shia Muslim, and so on. Similarly, Sunnis became divided into four groups: Hanafi, Shafiee, Maliki and Hanbali, but the followers of these four Sunni groups never identified themselves as sects. They still considered themselves Sunnis ("*Ahle Sunnah Wal Jama'h*", or the only group whose beliefs and teachings are truly in accordance with the Qur'an and Sunnah). The source of this division among Sunnis was the difference in the interpretation of the jurisprudence of Islam called the *Sharia Law*. The followers of these four Sunni groups (Mazahib) remained united on traditions and beliefs (Aqeedah) based upon the Imam Matarudi and Imam Ash'ari's understandings or interpretation of Islam. Even with all these divisions, Sunni scholars have never called each other "wrong." They have tended to be extremely tolerant and accepting of each other's differences. They have still prayed together and lived together in peace and harmony.

The Dangerous Division

Up to the 1700s, Sunni Muslims worldwide, had much the same beliefs and traditions but were divided on the issues of "*Fiqh*" (legal jurisprudence in Sharia law). During the 1700s and 1800s, when European powers invaded Asian and African countries to colonize them, the Khawrji beliefs were revived once again in Muslim countries in order to destroy the Ottoman Empire. Arab Nationalism and the violent ideology of Khawrjis were useful tools in aiding the European powers to divide Muslims and to pit them against each other. This strategy worked very well, and these European powers were successful in colonizing almost all Muslim countries.

The formation of Saudi Arabia took place during this same era. Ottoman Turkish rulers were the custodians of the two holy sites of Islam, but an alliance between a radical clergyman and a tribal chief of the Najd area, with the backing from Britain, defeated the Ottomans. Thus, Saudi Arabia was formed. The man of the clergy of Najd was Muhammad Bin Abdul Wahab. He revived the Khawrji beliefs and justified the killings of thousands of Muslims, just as the Khawarij had done when they killed thousands of companions and, the family members of Prophet Muhammad (PBUH), and "rationalized" their acts by employing their own interpretation of the Qur'an and Sunnah. Muhammad Bin Abdul Wahab demolished hundreds of the Islamic heritage sites that Muslims had lovingly preserved over the centuries as a part of Islam's history. He demolished thousands of tombs of various Sahabah and family members of the Prophet Muhammad (PBUH), which Muslims had built and protected throughout the history of Islam. He destroyed hundreds of historic archeological sites of Islam that had been preserved right from the period of the Prophet Muhammad (PBUH), by all Muslim governments and by all Muslims, until those sites were destroyed just less than a century ago. In fact, Muhammad Bin Abdul Wahab even wanted to demolish the "Rowdha" of the Prophet Muhammad (PBUH) where he was buried inside Masjid Al Nabawi in Madinah city.

At that time the entire community of Muslim scholars, both Shia and Sunni, condemned Muhammad Bin Abdul Wahab and his followers. No one accepted his interpretation of the Qur'an and Sunnah.

The Revival of Khawarijism

Today Muslims are struggling once again with challenges that are similar in many ways to those of the 1700s; however, the current challenges are even more serious and more impactful upon Muslims and on their faith, Islam. Today, the majority of Muslims are struggling with economic challenges. Nearly all Muslim countries are classed as "under-developed" – facing poverty, high rates of illiteracy and corrupt dictators. In addition, Saudi Arabia has become a strong economy in the world. Saudi Arabia is a member of the G20 countries, and one the closest allies of the United States, Canada and other western countries. Saudi Arabia also gives aid to many Muslim countries. Millions of Muslims and non-Muslims work in Saudi Arabia. The country has helped in rebuilding several countries after wars or natural disasters. It has also helped build thousands of mosques in the western world and in the Muslim world.

However, the Saudi help does not come without attachments. Economic and financial help from Saudi Arabia always has a price tag, and that price tag is the importation and adoption of Muhammad Bin Abdul Wahab's interpretation of Islam, known as *"Wahhabism"* or *"Salafism"*. *Wherever a mosque has been built with Saudi money, the Imam has had to be either imported from Saudi Arabia, educated in Saudi Arabia, OR a follower of the Wahhabi/Salafi version of Islam.*

Some Important Facts

Before the civil war in Bosnia Herzegovina, there were hardly any mosques that could be considered Wahhabi/Salafi Mosques. After the civil war ended, Saudi Arabia helped in rebuilding mosques and universities in Bosnia Herzegovina. Before the Afghan Jihad against the former Soviet Union, less than 20% of the mosques in Pakistan were Wahhabi/Salafi/Deobandi mosques. Saudi Arabia has provided extensive funding and Mujahideen through the government of General Ziaul Haq in Pakistan. Lots of money and lots of Saudi clergy came to Pakistan. Today more than 60% of the mosques in Pakistan are either Wahhabi/Salafi or Deobandi mosques. ("Deobandi" is another version of the Wahhabi/Salafi sect in South Asia). In other parts of the world such as central Asia, Indonesia, Malaysia, North Africa, and the Middle East, the Wahhabi / Salafi influence is on the rise exponentially. An overwhelming majority of Mosques in the United States and Canada have also received funding from Saudi Arabia. Therefore, the Wahhabi/Salafi influence in North American mosques is huge. Millions of Sunni Muslims who migrated from the various Muslim countries to North America were followers of non-Wahhabi Sunni schools of thoughts in their country of birth, but when they settled in the US or Canada they converted to the Wahhabi/Salafi sect. The reasons are obvious: the majority of mosques in North America are controlled, run and managed by Wahhabi/Salafi Imams and their followers. No other Sunni group has the kind of resources and the funding that Wahhabis have.

Moreover, since Islam's two holy sites, Makkah and Madinah, are in Saudi Arabia, millions of Muslims visit Saudi Arabia for pilgrimage (Hajj and Umrah). The majority of Muslims do not know the history of Islam and the history of the Wahhabi beliefs. The perception of most Muslims is that the clergy, which controls these two holy sites, must be correct. I wish they had been born 150 years ago. They would have seen a very different view of Islam and Islamic heritage sites in Makkah and Madinah when the Ottomans were ruling these cities. Millions of Muslims work in Saudi Arabia, and they certainly learn Islam from the Saudi clergy. They believe they are learning from the source. They do not know that the source has been contaminated.

Comparison

Let us compare some of the key differences between the beliefs of Sunni Muslims vs the Wahhabi / Salafi beliefs.

Sunni Muslim Beliefs (practiced by ALL Sunni Muslims for 1400 years of Islam).	**Wahhabi / Salafi Beliefs** (started after the Wahhabi revolution in Saudi Arabia less than 200 years ago).
Sunni Muslims have existed since the start of Islam more than 1400 years ago.	Wahhabis / Salafis (Khawarij) emerged for a short period of time during the Khilafah of Hazrat Osman and Imam Ali (May Allah be pleased with them). At that time, they used to be called *Khawarij*. They re-emerged in mid 1700s in the Arabian Peninsula.

All Sunni Muslims must follow one of the four Jurist Imams (Fiqh); Hanafi, Shafi'ee, Maliki &Hanbali.

Wahhabis / Salafis do not follow any of the four Imams of Fiqh.

All Sunni Muslims believe in the intercession of Prophet Muhammad (PBUH) on the judgement day.

Wahhabis / Salafis do not believe in the intercession (Shifa'h) of Prophet Muhammad (PBUH).

All Sunni Muslims believe in "Tawassul" (mediation) to Allah

Wahhabis / Salafis do not believe in Tawassul.

All Sunni Muslims believe in celebrating the birthday of Prophet Muhammad (PBUH) called "Eid Milad un Nabi". The formal celebration of Prophet Muhammad's (PBUH) birthday started 250 -300 years after he passed away. Since then All Muslims, Shia and Sunni, have celebrates Eid Milad un Nabi (PBUH). No single scholar of Islam ever objected to this celebration. All Muslim countries celebrate this day as a national holiday except Saudi Arabia and Qatar.

Wahhabis / Salafis do not believe in celebrating Eid Milad un Nabi (PBUH). They consider this a Bid'a (innovation in Islam). If anyone ever tries to celebrate Eid Milad un Nabi (PBUH) in Saudi Arabia publicly, the person will be prosecuted, jailed and/or deported. It's a crime in Saudi Arabia. That is why Wahhabis /Salafis consider a person an infidel if he/she celebrates Prophet Muhammad's birthday (PBUH).

All Sunni Muslims praise and honour Prophet Muhammad (PBUH) by singing poems and rhymes (Naat & Nasheed)	Praising and honouring Prophet Muhammad (PBUH) pains Wahhabis / Salafis.
All Sunni Muslims respect and accept differences of opinions. For Sunni Muslims the followers of all four Fiqh Imams; Hanafi, Maliki, Shafi'ee and Hanbali were correct and must be respected, although they differ from each other on many rulings of Islamic law.	Wahhabi / Salafi cannot tolerate any disagreement or difference of opinions. They believe they are the only true Muslims and all other Muslims are pagans, non-believers or hell-bound.
All Sunni Muslims love Aulia Allah (Sufis of Islam) and visit their graves.	Wahhabis / Salafis hate Sufis. Visiting graves of Aulia Allah is "shirk" (paganism) for them.
It is every Muslim's lifetime desire to visit the Rowdah (grave) of Prophet Muhammad (PBUH) in Masjid Al Nabawi in Madinah city.	Wahhabis / Salafis consider this to be shirk. They say one can go to Masjid Al Nabwi to pray, and no one should have the intention to visit the Rowdah of Prophet Muhammad (PBUH)
All Sunni Muslims believe in the sanctity of life, whether Muslim or non-Muslim. Killing innocent men, women and children (Muslim or non-Muslim) is a major sin and crime in Islam.	Wahhabis / Salafi believe in the forceful conversion of non-Muslims. Anyone who refuses their authority and judgement is subject to death, Muslim or non-Muslim.

So what must New Converts do?

The problem is confusing and serious. When a person goes to a mosque, or meets an Imam to convert to Islam, that person often does not know the beliefs and the sect of the Imam. A Wahhabi / Salafi NEVER calls himself/herself a "Wahhabi / Salafi". They call themselves "true Muslims." Khawarij never considered themselves to be outsiders of Islam, either. In fact, they expelled every other Muslim from the Islamic fold and took over the ownership of Islam. Wahhabis/Salafis call themselves "true Muslims", and consider all other Muslims to be either pagans or damned. So, how can a person who wants to embrace Islam ensure that he/she is really embracing Islam, and not Wahhabism/Salafism disguised as Islam?

The answer is very simple. Check the Imam or the person who is going to teach you Islam as to whether he/she believes according to the Sunni beliefs, or the beliefs of Wahhabi/Salafi sect. You should not be misguided by the Wahhabis/Salafis and later be recruited to fight for that most dangerous of terrorist groups, the Wahhabi/Salafi organization called *"ISIS"* or *"ISIL"*.

The checklist

Please ask the following questions to the Imam or the person helping you to understand Islam.

a. Do you agree Islam protects the sanctity of life for all human beings, including Christians, Jews and others?

b. Do you believe Muslims can live in peace and harmony with Christians and Jews?

c. Do you stand up to protect the rights of non-Muslim minorities in Muslim countries?

d. Do you agree Muslims who were recruited by ISIL/ISIS were misled and radicalized?

e. Do you write and speak against the ideology of such groups as ISIS/ISIL, Boko Haram, Al Qaeda, and the Taliban? Do you agree their ideology, beliefs and actions are criminal and completely un-Islamic?

f. Do you agree that, in Islam, that no individual or a group can declare armed Jihad against anyone?

g. Do you agree Muslims must be loyal law-abiding citizens of the countries they live in?

h. Do you believe, in Islam, that men and women have equal rights?

i. Do you believe honour killings are un-Islamic and major crimes in Islam?

j. Do you consider forced and underage marriages to be un-Islamic?

k. Do you believe non-Muslims in Muslim countries should be forced to become Muslims?

l. Do you believe Muslims of other sects will go to hell unless they follow your beliefs?

m. Do you call other Muslims who may disagree with your beliefs and traditions "Kafir" (non-believer), "Mushrik" (pagans) or "Bid'atee" (innovators)?

The answers for questions 1 -10 should be **YES**. Answers for questions 11-13 should be **NO**.

Conclusion

I also request that the media, law enforcement agencies, government officials *NOT* refer to groups like ISIS/ISIL, Al Qaeda, Taliban, Al Shabab, Boko Haram, Al Nusrah, Khorasan, etc. as "Sunni Muslims." All these terrorist organizations, their members and sympathizers, are the followers of Wahhabism/Salafism. They must be identified with their correct affiliation. They are not Sunni Muslims.

If any brother or sister who would like to embrace Islam and need help you can contact me at 1-416-994-5467 OR email: contact@islamicsupremecouncil.com, or at www.iscc.ca.

Open Letters

Date: April 12, 2003

Honourable Kings, Presidents and Rulers of Muslim Countries

Assalamo Alaikum wa Rahmatullah wa Barakatuh

The recent fall of one of your colleagues, Saddam Hussein and his regime, has been an important lesson for all the rulers of the Muslim world. As Almighty Allah says in the Glorious Qur'an, **Hence, take a lesson O the people possessing insight (59: 2).** Earlier, you saw the disgraced and humiliated fall of King Raza Shah of Iran, Idi Ameen of Uganda, President Suharto of Indonesia, and several other rulers of the Muslim and non-Muslim worlds. These rulers never imagined that such humiliation and destruction would fall upon them. You, too, are not immune to such humiliation and destruction? Today, you may be in "the good books" of the American government, but you can be removed from this favoured position at any time. The US government will never let American interest sacrificed in favour of yours or your country's interests. For the American governments, Muslims and Muslim governments have been and will always be like a paper napkin, to be applied to the eyes or cheeks when needed, but thrown into the trash once it's soiled or torn. What makes you think that, sooner or later, you will not be "trashed" by the US?

As Allah reminds Muslims in the Glorious Qur'an, **And such are the days We alternate among human beings (3:140).** Please do not be foolish like Saddam Hussein. Please learn from history.

The only way you (the current Muslim rulers) can avoid destruction and forceful removal from power, regardless of whether you are a US ally or opponent, is by acknowledging the *TRUTH.*

---

o   Is it not true that most of you have huge palaces like Saddam Hussein, while most of the people in your countries live in substandard houses or on the streets? I have seen miles and miles of long palaces in Muslim countries while widows and orphans begged in the downtown areas of the same city.

o   Is it not true that you enjoy the most luxurious lifestyle on earth, while an overwhelming majority of your citizens are deprived of basic human needs, just as it was with Saddam Hussein and the people of Iraq?

o   Is it not true that you and the people of your "inner circles" use your countries' resources without any accountability, while the ordinary citizens in your countries are accountable for everything?

o   Is it not true that you cannot tolerate any opposition in your country, just like Saddam Hussein could not tolerate any opposition?

o   Is it not true that most of you have imposed yourselves upon your people, like Saddam Hussein did?

o   Is it not true that most of you are elected through fake elections (one man, one party referendum), in the same way as Saddam Hussein used to be elected?

o   Is it not true that most of you have killed or sent in exile, hundreds of citizens who tried to challenge your rule?

o   Is it not true that some of you have established parliaments because of western pressure but the actual power has remained in your hands? The parliaments are only for symbolic purposes.

o   Is it not true that you have manifested all powers and authorities in yourselves?

o   Is it not true that in your countries, the laws made by you supersede the laws given to Muslims by Almighty Allah (Qur'an) and His Messenger (PBUH)?

o   Is it not true that the "justice" for an ordinary person is different from the justice for a privileged person in your countries?

o   Is it not true that when a poor person commits a wrong, he/she is punished to the fullest extent of the law, while a wrong committed by a privileged person in your countries frequently goes unnoticed?

Therefore, eventually your fate will be no different from Saddam Hussein's, unless you repent and fear ONLY Almighty Allah and establish justice and freedom for the ordinary citizens of your countries.

Let me ask you a question. Why did the US forces face humiliation and defeat in Vietnam? Please compare Saddam Hussein and yourselves with Ho Chi Min. Ho Chi Min did not have large palaces. His standard of living was similar to that of an average Vietnamese at that time. He "empowered" ordinary citizens. That is why all the old and the young, men and women, became, in effect, part of the North Vietnamese army defending their country. In order to have truly occupied the whole of Vietnam, the American forces would have had to kill each North Vietnamese. That is why the American forces failed there.

In the case of Iraq, ordinary citizens had been robbed and oppressed by Saddam for years. Why would they fight for such a tyrant? Please be honest with yourselves. You have the same situation in your countries. May Allah keep all Muslims countries safe; however, reality is already knocking at the door. People will not fight for you. Your elite armies may be able to fight for a few days and that is it. In order to keep your honour and your country safe, please do the following. Then you will see how ordinary citizens will stand-up and defend the country against any aggression, and how Almighty Allah will help you and your country.

▪   Withdraw all the laws that conflict with the Divine laws of Islamic Shari'a. Fear only Allah. Love Allah's Messenger (PBUH) more than anything else and respect ordinary human beings.

- Establish in your country a transparent justice system for all, including for the non-Muslim minorities. Allah may tolerate a non-Muslim government with justice, but will not tolerate a Muslim government without justice (Imam Ibn Taymiyah).

- Let the people choose their leader or ruler through unrestricted, uncontrolled and fair elections.

- Convert all those large palaces and huge government buildings into housing projects for the homeless and the poor. Give back people's money and respect human rights.

- Empower ordinary citizens. Let them enjoy Allah's given freedom.

- Your standard of living should be similar to that of an average citizen of your country. And above all:

- *You should like for yourselves what you like for others.*

- Unite Muslim countries. Instead of dividing yourselves into the Arab League, ICO, GCC and other useless organizations. Establish your own United Nations of Islamic Countries (UNIC). The current UNO has lost its face and its value. The current UNO cannot protect poor countries from the aggression of powerful countries.

Honourable Kings, Presidents and Rulers of the Muslim Countries,

Soon, another Muslim country will be facing aggression and if you do not change, change will be forced upon you, just as it was in Afghanistan and Iraq. This imposed change will be very destructive, as you have seen in Iraq and Afghanistan.

Muslims must establish Khilafah. This will require sacrifices from the Muslim rulers. The unity of the Muslim Ummah is only in establishing the Khilafah. Unless Muslims are united, the occupation of Muslim countries and the genocide of Muslims will continue.

The model rulers for all of you is Muhammad (PBUH) and Khilafat-e-Rashidah. Remember, when Ameer-ul-Mo'mineen, Sayyidna Umar ibn Al-Khattab (May Allah be pleased with him) entered into Jerusalem as the Commander-in-Chief of the victorious Muslim army. He walked beside his camel, and his slave rode on the camel. He showed the utmost respect for the people of all Faiths in Jerusalem. We need Salahuddin Ayyubi (May Allah shower His blessings upon him), a Kurd by background, who defeated the Crusaders and re-captured Jerusalem from them. If you want to succeed like Sayyidna Umar ibn Al-Khattab and Sayyidna Salahuddin Ayyubi, you must adopt their values and lifestyle.

Let me remind you and myself, Allah says in the Glorious Qur'an: **Whoever recommends and helps a good cause becomes a partner therein: and whoever recommends and helps an evil cause shares in its burden: and Allah has power over all things (4:85)**

O who believe! if you comply with who disbelieve, they shall turn you back and then, you shall turn losers. On the contrary, Allah is your protector: and He is the best helper. (3: 149-150)

You must neither flag (lose vigour) nor grieve and you shall have victory, if you are (true) believers. (3: 139)

May Allah keep the world in peace from the tyrants of the East and the West. Amen.

Thank you,

****

Date: November 28, 2002

Rev. Pat Robertson

The Christian Broadcasting Network
977 Centerville Turnpike
Virginia Beach, VA 23463

Re: Open letter to Rev. Pat Robertson

Rev. Pat Robertson,

On November 26, 2002 you gave an interview to Martin Savidge of CNN. Your interview proves that you certainly need help. I am sure you realize that telling a lie is a sin in Christianity. In your interview you tried to misguide and misinform people by making inaccurate remarks about "Jihad" and the peaceful nature of Islam. Just reading a translation of the Qur'an and quoting it's verses out of context is hugely dishonest and immoral.

Without going into details, I would like to ask you the following questions. I am sure you know the answers of these questions. These facts are in the history books written by Christian authors.

Who killed thousands of aboriginal people in North America and Australia in order to occupy their lands and properties?

1. Who killed millions of South Americans and forced them to Christianity?

2. Who killed millions of human beings in World War I?

3. Who killed 6 million Jews during World War II?

4. Who killed 2 million Polish Christians in World War II?

5. Who killed 6 million Chinese during the invasion of China?

6. Who killed 2 million Cambodians during the civil war of the 1970s?

7. Who killed more than 2 million Filipinos during the invasion of Philippines?

8. Who killed more than half a million Tibetans during the last 6 decades?

9. Who killed more than 2 million Vietnamese during the Vietnam War?
10. Who dropped chemical and biological bombs on Vietnam?
11. Who dropped nuclear bombs on Japan and killed thousands of people in Hiroshima and Nagasaki?
12. Who killed more than 2 million African Christians in Rwanda, Sierra Leone, Burundi and Congo within the last two decades?
13. Who made more than 9.5 million human beings refugees in Africa?
14. Who is killing and confiscating lands from White farmers in Zimbabwe?
15. Who invented nuclear, biological and chemical bombs?
16. Who sells the most sophisticated bombs and the best killing machines to the world?
17. Who killed hundreds of blacks in America and did not consider them full human beings until the 1960s?
18. Who are the "White Supremacists"?
19. Who did not officially consider women as persons until the 1940s?

I am purposely not asking you about the killings of millions of Muslims in Bosnia, Kosovo, Chechnya, Kashmir, Palestine, Russian Federation, Iraq, Afghanistan, China, India, etc.

Can you please prove that the most of the abovementioned mass killings of humans were not caused by the people who claimed to be Christians? Were Non-Muslims not also perpetrators of the other incidents of genocide mentioned? If you are interested, I can send you a more extensive, detailed list of all the holocausts and genocides caused by people who claimed to be Christians.

Rev. Robertson, I propose that you and I have a dialogue. You should bring a list of all the killings carried out by the Muslims throughout the history and I will bring a list of all the killings caused by the Christians, and let us compare both lists. I am confident I can prove that the killings carried out by the Muslims are negligible compared to the killings carried out by Christians and other non-Muslims.

On behalf of Islamic Supreme Council of Canada (ISCC), I would like to invite you to visit Canada, and we will arrange an open town hall meeting to discuss your issues with Islam. ISCC will pay all your travel and lodging expenses. If this is not possible for you, please let me know when and where you can meet with me to have a dialogue and I will travel to your place at my own expense.

I strongly believe in bringing together the followers of Christianity, Islam and Judaism. These three great religions have more commonalities than differences, but people like you are destroying these efforts.

Rev. Robertson, your ignorance about the Qur'an, Prophet Muhammad (PBUH) and Islam is so deep that you do not even know the basic beliefs of a Muslim. You do not even know how to spell Qur'an (it is not "Koran", it is "Qur'an"). We are here to help you. We, as Muslims do not hate God's creation. It is a requirement of our faith that we like for others what we like for ourselves. We just want to educate you about Islam so that you can be a better person.

In the past we have asked Rev. Franklin Graham, Rev. Jerry Falwell and other Christian leaders to attend our course, Islam 101 in Toronto and ask as many questions as they wanted about Islam and Muslims. But please do not badmouth about our religion in the media. We do not have access to the media as you do. We, the Muslims living in Canada and the USA, know that the media in North America is NOT FREE. In the third world countries, the dictators and the governments control the media, while the Western media is controlled by rich and strong interest groups. Had the media in the west been free, Muslim leaders would have gotten an equal chance to respond to the comments made by the people like yourself.

I am looking forward to hearing from you soon. Season's greetings to you and to your family and friends.

Thanks

****

Date: November 19, 2001

Dear Rev. Franklin Graham,

As per the following media reports, the Canadian Muslims are concerned that a knowledgeable person like yourself does not know or understand the teachings of Islam. Let me quote from the following two media reports before going further.

In a report aired Friday on "NBC Nightly News," Rev. Franklin Graham stood by remarks he made about Islam last month at the dedication of a chapel in North Carolina. At that event, Graham said:

> "We're not attacking Islam but Islam has attacked us. The God of Islam is not the same God. He's not the son of God of the Christian or Judeo-Christian faith. It's a different God, and I believe it is a very evil and wicked religion." In the NBC report, Graham said, "I don't believe this [Islam] is this wonderful, peaceful religion."

> (See: http://www.msnbc.com/news/659057.asp?cp1=1)

On Sunday, Graham issued a statement in which he said:

> "It is not my calling to analyze Islam or any other religions, though I recognize that all religions have differences. In the past, I have expressed my concerns about the teachings of Islam regarding the treatment of women and the killing of non-Muslims or infidels." Graham said he would have no further comments on the issue.

> (See:
> http://www.charlotte.com/observer/natwor/docs/franklin
> 1119.htm)

I saw your father, the Reverend Billy Graham (for whom I have the deepest respect) on TV at the National Day of Prayer and Remembrance service at the National Cathedral in Washington, on Sept. 14, saying, "We come together today to affirm our conviction that God cares for us, whatever our ethnic, religious or political background may be," He further said, "The Bible says that He is `the God of all comfort, who comforts us in all our troubles.'"

You must have some misunderstandings about the teachings of Islam, and we are sure that these misunderstandings can be dispelled through dialogue. Therefore, on behalf of ISCC, I would like to invite you to visit Calgary and discuss all the issues which you might have with the Islamic faith. ISCC will pay all your travel and living expenses to Calgary. Please choose a date and time convenient for you and let us know. If your busy schedule does not allow you to come to Calgary I am willing to travel to any place where we can discuss your issues with Islam. Please let me know when do you have some time to meet with me at a place of your choice.

Thank you very much and looking forward to hearing from you soon.

****

Note: The next letter was sent to Mullah Umar before United States attacked Afghanistan after the tragedy of 9-11.

Date: October 3, 2001

Open Letter to Mullah Umar

Honourable Mullah Umar

Ameer of Taliban

Kabul, Afghanistan

Honourable Mullah Umar,

As a Muslim I felt obligated to write to you and share with you my thoughts about the current situation in and around Afghanistan. To be honest with you, I have never supported the Taliban style of implementing and preaching Islam. But you may agree with me that this is the beauty of our religion, namely: that an ordinary Muslim like myself and a Muslim like you who is Head of State of a Muslim country can respectfully disagree with each other. This is the way the Companions of Prophet Muhammad (PBUH) ruled the Islamic State for many years. I hope and pray that my letter will reach out to you before things gets worse. I do not want to make this letter very long. I just wanted to remind you of two very important, critical treaties of Islamic history which apparently appeared at that time to be very humiliating and insulting for Muslims, but Allah had turned those incidents into victories for Muslims.

The first was the treaty of Hudaibiyah which Prophet Muhammad (PBUH) signed with the Quraish (Pagans) of Makkah during 6 A.H. Two things in that treaty were highly disturbing for the Muslims, the first and the fourth conditions, which they said were expressly unfair. With reference to the first: if they had to return a fugitive from Makkah, why should not the Quraish return a fugitive from Madinah? To this the Holy Prophet replied: "What use would be he to us, who fled from us to them? May Allah keep him away from us! And if we return the one who flees to us from them, Allah will create some other way out for him." The fourth condition rankled as well. The Muslims thought that agreeing to it meant they would return unsuccessful and this was humiliating. Furthermore, the question that caused them upset was that they had to accept the condition of going back without performing the pilgrimage to the Ka'bah. According to the treaty conditions, they would have to perform the pilgrimage the following year, if it pleased Allah.

Right at the time when the document was being written, Suhail bin 'Amr's (the leader of pagans') own son, Abu Jandal, who had become a Muslim and been imprisoned by the pagans of Makkah, somehow escaped to the Holy Prophet's camp. He had fetters on his feet and signs of violence on his body. He implored the Holy Prophet to help secure his release from imprisonment. The scene only increased the Companions' dejection, and they were moved beyond control. But Suhail bin 'Amr said the conditions of the agreement had been concluded between them although the writing was not yet complete; therefore, the boy should be returned to them. The Holy Prophet admitted his argument and Abu Jandal was returned to his oppressors.

A Second incident took place in the nineteenth year after the Hijrah. Umar ibn Al Khattab, second Caliph of Islam, (May Allah be pleased with him) dispatched an army to fight against the Byzantine Empire. In it was Abdullah ibn Hudhafah. News of the Muslim force reached the Byzantine emperor. He had heard of their sincerity of faith, and their willingness to sacrifice their lives in the way of God and His Prophet. He gave orders to his men to bring to him any Muslim captive they might take alive.

God willed that Abdullah ibn Hudhafah should fall captive to the Byzantines and he was brought before the Emperor. The Emperor looked at Abdullah for a long time. Suddenly he said, "I shall make a proposal to you." "What is it?" asked Abdullah. "I suggest that you become a Christian. If you do this, you will be set free and I shall grant you a safe refuge." The prisoner's reaction was furious: "Death is preferable to me a thousand times to what you ask me to do."

"I see that you are a bold man. However, if you respond positively to what I propose to you, I will give you a share in my authority and swear you in as my aide."

The prisoner, shackled in his chains, smiled and said, "By God, if you give me all that you possess and all that the Arabs have in exchange for giving up the religion of Muhammad, I shall not do so."

"Then I shall kill you."

"Do what you want," answered Abdullah.

The emperor then had him put on a cross and ordered his soldiers to throw spears near him, first near his hands and then near his feet, all the while telling him to accept Christianity or at least give up his religion. This he refused over and over again to do.

The emperor then had him taken down from the wooden cross. He called for a great pot to be brought. This was filled with oil, which was then heated under a fierce fire. He then had two other Muslim prisoners brought and had one of them thrown into the boiling oil. The prisoner's flesh sizzled and soon his bones could be seen. The emperor turned to Abdullah and invited him to Christianity.

This was the most terrible test that Abdullah had to face up till now. But he remained firm and the emperor gave up trying. He then ordered that Abdullah too be thrown into the pot. As he was being taken away he began to shed tears. The emperor thought that he had at last been broken and had him brought back to him. He once more suggested that Abdullah become a Christian but to his astonishment, Abdullah refused.

"Damn you! Why did you weep then?" shouted the emperor.

"I cried," said Abdullah, "because I said to myself 'You will now be thrown into this pot and your soul will depart'. What I really desired then was to have as many souls as the number of hairs on my body and to have all of them thrown into this pot for the sake of God."

The tyrant then said, "Will you kiss my head? I will then set you free."

"And all the Muslim prisoners also?" asked Abdullah.

This the emperor agreed to do and Abdullah said to himself, "One of the enemies of God! I shall kiss his head and he shall set me and all other Muslim prisoners free. There can be no blame on me for doing this." He then went up to the emperor and kissed his forehead. All the Muslim prisoners were released and handed over to Abdullah.

Abdullah ibn Hudhafah eventually came to Umar ibn al-Khattab (May Allah be pleased with him) and told him what had happened. Umar was greatly pleased and when he looked at the prisoners he said, "Every Muslim has a duty to kiss the head of Abdullah ibn Hudhafah and I shall start." Umar then got up and kissed the head of Abdullah ibn Hudhafah. Had Abdullah ibn Hudhafah been stubborn and not kissed the head of enemy of Islam he would have died along with many other Muslims. But he was a smart and sincere Muslim. He saved himself and saved many other Muslims too.

I fully understand and recognize that you are an Islamic scholar, but at the same time Islam has given me the right to express my opinion freely and openly even in front of a Head of State. During the period of the four Caliphs of Islam, an ordinary person could stop Ameer-ul-Mo'mineen on the street and challenge him for his decisions or actions. I am using the same right and asking you to consider that your decision, not to hand over Osama Bin Laden to the United States, is wrong. One Muslim's interest must not be preferred over the interest of the entire Muslim Ummah. Osama Bin Laden is not only a suspect in the terrorist bombings in Tanzania and Kenya. He is also a suspect for the September 11, 2001 terrorist attacks in New York and Washington D.C. No doubt, these crimes are against the teachings of Islam and I know you have also condemned these attacks.

Honourable Mullah Umar,

I know it is very painful for Osama bin Laden to be in the hands of his enemies, but please consider him like Abu Jandal (May Allah be pleased with him) and hand-over Osama to the USA as the Prophet Muhammad (PBUH) handed over Abu Jandal to Quraish. Consider yourself as Abdullah ibn Hudhafah (May Allah be pleased with him). Kiss the head of today's Byzantine Emperor (George Bush) and save your own and millions of lives of other Muslims.

If you still think that you can fight with the USA and its allied forces, I would say nothing but to tell you of one more noble incident of our beloved Prophet and his very sincere and beloved Companion Abu Dhar Ghaffari (May Allah be pleased with him). Once, Allah's Messenger (PBUH) was appointing various governors for various territories of the Islamic State. Abu Dhar Ghaffari (May Allah be pleased with) went to Allah's Messenger and said, O' Allah's Messenger you are appointing different governors, may I also be appointed as a governor of some Islamic territory? As you also know, the Prophet Muhammad (PBUH) loved Abu Dhar Ghaffari very much. He was one of the most pious, sincere and beloved companions of Allah's Messenger. However, Allah's Messenger (PBUH) told Abu Dhar that to be a ruler of a state or territory required some special skills and characteristics which he (Abu Dhar) did not have and he did not appoint him. This proves that for a ruler, it is not enough to be a pious and a practicing Muslim. Along with piety and knowledge, the position requires some very special decision making, diplomacy skills, and a different way of thinking, which you do not, seem to have. You may be very good Muslim but this may not be enough to qualify you to be a ruler.

In short, in order to be victorious in the battle of Badr, it is mandatory for Muslims to go through the training – miseries and humiliation of Makkah. The present period in our history is similar to the Makkan life of early Muslims.

Who brought back this period of humiliation and miseries upon Muslims? This period of humiliations and miseries was brought upon us by those so-called Muslims who fought against the Islamic Superpower, Khilafat-e-Islamiyah (the Ottoman Empire) during the 1700 and 1800s in the Najd area which is now a part of Saudi Arabia. They founded a new ideology in the name of Islam called Wahhabism. Using this new ideology they fought against Muslims and destroyed Khilafat-e-Islamiyah. Wahhabism is based upon hate, killing and destruction, while Islam is based upon love, life and construction. You are in the trap of Wahhabism and you need to remove yourself and your followers from this trap. May Allah help us and make us good Muslims. Ameen.

I said what I understood is right. The true knowledge is with Allah.

Thank you and Jazakumullah-o-khairan

Date: September 18, 2001

The Right Hon. Jean Chrétien

Prime Minister of Canada

Parliament Hill

Ottawa, Ontario, Canada

K1A 0A4

The Right Hon. Jean Chrétien,

On behalf of Muslims Against Terrorism (MAT) and the Islamic Supreme Council of Canada (ISCC), I would like to draw your attention towards a crisis, which may get worse with time. I am sure you are aware of the current situation faced by Canadian Muslims. Since the September 11 terrorists' attacks in New York and Washington D.C., Canadian Muslims have been the targets of hate, violence, intimidation and discrimination. There have been several incidents in various parts of the country where the mosques have been vandalized, Muslim students in universities and schools have been harassed, Muslim women have been intimidated and death threats have been made to Muslim families. Personally, I have received four death threats on my own phone. I have reported those messages to the police and they are conducting an investigation.

I am sure you will agree that Canadian Muslims are as Canadian as anybody else is. Canadian Muslims pay taxes just like other Canadians. Canadian Muslims are working and contributing to the Canadian economy as any other Canadian. But I am not sure why Canadian Muslims become targets of hate and violence in the case of any terrorism act? Is it because we follow a different religion from mainstream Canadians? Is it because of our ethnicity, or is it because of our colour and dress? When any terrorist commits a crime why do all Muslims have to face persecution? Why do Muslims have to defend themselves and explain again and again that they are peace-loving citizens of this country?

If an individual or a group of individuals who happen to claim they are Muslims commit a crime in the name of Islam, it does not follow that all the Muslims are like them. There are terrorists and extremists in other religions, too. I do not think I need to identify them in this letter. Why are the terrorists and criminals of other religions not identified and associated with their religions? Why have only Muslims been singled out? Please forgive me but I have to say that Canada is still far away from being a just society. However, we all need to work together to achieve that goal.

We have explained and informed the public many times that Islam means peace. Our holy book, the Qur'an tells us that killing one person is as killing all mankind and saving one human life is as saving all mankind. The Prophet Muhammad (PBUH) has given us a very clear definition of a Muslim. He (PBUH) said," A Muslim is that person from whose hands and tongue the others are safe ". Terrorism has no place in the Muslim community. Killing innocent people, regardless of their religion, race and colour, is a major sin in Islam.

God's Last Messenger towards humanity, Muhammad (PBUH) has told us that even in the situation of a war, do not kill children, do not kill women, do not kill old men, do not kill sick, do not cut trees, do not contaminate water, do not destroy the places of worship of other religions, do not kill animals except for food. Where in the world can we get a better code of conduct than Islam?

Muslims *do* condemn the September 11 terrorist attacks on United States. On September 11, 2001 ISCC and MAT sent you and the Canadian and US media the strongest condemnation of those terrorists' attacks. We demand that the US government punish those terrorists and their supporters responsible for the WTC and Pentagon disasters. But this punishment should not be given to the innocent and poor children, women and families of Muslim countries like Afghanistan, Iraq and Lebanon.

The Right Honourable Prime Minister,

After September 11, we, Canadian Muslims, have not felt secure and safe in Canada. Our women and children are facing humiliation and intimidation in Canada. We cannot practice our religion freely. In USA there have been two murders and numerous cases of vandalism and harassment. These trends are slowly moving towards Canada. We are certain that when American and NATO forces attack Muslim countries, the hostilities against Canadian Muslims will increase. The risk of violence against Muslims is very high. As our Prime Minister, we would like to ask you what actions have you taken to make sure that the Canadian Muslims do not become victims of another form of terrorism caused by our own neighbours and fellow citizens. Did the Canadian government make sure that when a Muslim country was attacked by the US and NATO forces, the children, the women, hospitals, mosques, schools and other peace loving Muslims of that country would not be harmed? Can we rely on you and your government to see that no Canadian Muslim and peace-loving Muslims in Afghanistan, Iraq, etc. will be harmed? Please let us know.

The Right Honourable Prime Minister,

On behalf of the Islamic Supreme Council of Canada (ISCC), Muslims Against Terrorism (MAT) and all Canadian Muslims, I would like to mention that the Canadian government has miserably failed in educating its citizens about the values, beliefs and cultures of the Muslim community. Although, the Canadian government claims that Canada is a multicultural society, I am sorry to say that this is nothing more than lip service. Canada cannot be multicultural unless all Canadians tolerate, respect and understand the beauty of having different religions, languages, ethnicity, cultures and colours in Canada. The Canadian government has failed to promote true multiculturalism based upon mutual respect, tolerance and justice. Having a few bureaucrats and some departments in the government to promote multiculturalism is absolutely not enough. The ordinary citizens of Canada need to be active participants in multiculturalism and have enough understanding of other religions and cultures.

In order to minimize any possibility of future violence against Muslims and visible minorities, we would like to propose the following short term and long term actions.

Short Term Actions:

ISCC and MAT request that you;

1. Please address Canadians through public media and ask them to refrain from violence against Muslims and visible minorities. Canadian should be informed that the Muslims are also equal citizens of Canada and as loyal as white Christian Canadians.

2. Ask provincial and municipal governments to increase the security level in the cities and towns. Provide police protection to Muslim owned businesses, mosques and Islamic schools.

3. Ask Canadian media not to use words such as "Muslim terrorist, Islamic terrorist, Muslim extremist, Islamic extremist, Muslim fundamentalist, Islamic fundamentalist," and the like. Such things do not exist, and these words create hate and violence towards Muslims and the religion of Islam.

4. Pass a resolution in the house of commons condemning terrorist attacks on the United States and asking Canadians to stay united against the forces of division, hate and intolerance.

5. Long Term Actions:

6. Religious and cultural studies should be included in school curricula. In this course, children should learn about the beliefs, traditions and teachings of all major religions of the world, including Islam.

7. The participation of Muslim scholars and intellectuals in the media is minimal, compared to the followers of Christianity and Judaism. Islam is the second largest religion in Canada, but its representation in the media is the lowest. Laws should be made in order to ensure that the Muslims and the other visible minorities get equal opportunity in media reporting activities and programs.

8. The Federal government should announce a **National Diversity Day**. On this national day, people of all faiths and cultures should celebrate their heritage and express their unity as one Canadian nation.

I would also like to request you that the Federal government should organize a **"National Counter Terrorism Conference"** and invite leaders of religious and ethnic communities in Canada to discuss and plan Counter Terrorism. If the Federal government is unable to organize such a conference, the Islamic Supreme Council of Canada and the Muslims Against Terrorism would be pleased to organize this conference. Depending upon your availability, we will be more than happy to organize this conference in any part of Canada, on a date and time convenient for you. Please let us know.

Thanks

****

Date: October 5, 2001

Honourable George W. Bush

President

United States of America

Washington D.C., USA

Dear Mr. President,

On behalf of Muslims Against Terrorism (MAT), I would like to inform you that the worldwide membership of MAT has expressed their solidarity with the victims of the September 11, 2001 terrorist attacks on WTC and the Pentagon. These cowardly acts of terrorism have no place in the Muslim community, and we request that you find those terrorists and punish them. I understand that these terrorist attacks have forced you and the American government to wage a war against terrorism. The American government has allocated more than $40 billion to fight against terrorism at a time when the economy is on a downturn and economic recession is knocking at the door.

Unfortunately, in this chaos, the approach which US government has taken to combat terrorism may not be as useful as expected. The current strategy and approach to combat terrorism may create more terrorists and generate more violence.

Mr. President,

Upon completion of your term for the presidency you will be gone from the White House, but the policies and directions you will give to the American forces will have very long lasting impacts on this world. I do care for the stability, prosperity and security of North America. It affects me, my family, all Canadians, Americans, Muslims, Christians, Jews and the whole world. Therefore, it is important for me to share some of my thoughts with you.

Mr. President,

It is possible that we may not be able to eliminate violence and terrorism from this world, but we must be able to reduce it significantly. Merely capturing and punishing a few terrorists and destroying their networks will not solve the problem. The minimization of terrorism is only possible when we are able to remove the causes of terrorism. In my opinion, there are two major causes, or sources of terrorism. The first cause is the hypocrisy of the elite (privileged) class in worldwide society. The second cause or source of terrorism is the lack of communication and understanding among the ordinary (unprivileged) people of the worldwide community. I do consider the governments of the United States and the developed world as an elite (privileged) class in the worldwide society. In this short letter, I cannot analyse all the details of the policies and behaviour of the American government towards the unprivileged worldwide community, but I would like to highlight few of them.

The most important thing for Americans is their freedom, freedom of expression, freedom of lifestyle, freedom of choosing their government, etc. However, the American government does not want the people in the Muslim countries to enjoy the same freedom of expression, freedom to choose their own government and freedom to choose their lifestyle. The proof of this statement lies in the fact that the US government supports the harshly autocratic and dictatorial governments in Muslim countries. The people in the Muslim world are oppressed by these dictators and see that the only ally these dictators have is the US government. Why does the US government want to be with the bad guys?

The freedom of choice is an integral part of American society. The democratic principles of the American constitution demand that the government of United States respect the opinion of the majority of the people. Let us assume a hypothetical situation (I have to use a hypothetical situation because these situations do not exist in the USA, but are very real outside the USA.) If the people in the State of Texas decide that they do not want to be a part of the union. Will you call the national army and deploy them on every street of Texas, kill as many innocent civilians as possible so that the demographics of the state could be changed, use air power and carpet-bomb the State? I am sure you would say "NO!" The government of the USA would respect the people's opinion. But when a similar, REAL situation occurs in Palestine, Chechnya, Kashmir, and other parts of the world, the American governments has apparently not wanted to respect people's opinion. The US government supports the oppressive governments. Why have the people of countries like Palestine, Kashmir and Chechnya been made hostages against their will?

Over the last two three centuries, western society has gone through tremendous changes. It had opportunities to go through a process of change allowing it to set up the standards and choose its own destiny. On the other hand, after more than two centuries of imperialism in many Muslim countries, although the people of those countries want to set their own standards and choose their own destiny as well, they are not allowed to do so. They have always been told what to do? Who can be their friend and who cannot be their friend is decided by the American government. The IMF, the World Bank, the CIA, and other external bodies also make the crucial decisions about their policies and governments. These countries are not free to make their own decisions. The grip of IMF, World Bank and the CIA is getting tighter and tighter on Muslim countries. Because of this constricting situation, some people have taken an extreme side, and have become the reason for violence and terrorism.

Mr. President, what is terrorism? When these Taliban were fighting under the supervision of the Americans against the Russians, they were called freedom fighters. America supported them and harboured them. During the 1980s, when Saddam Hussain was using chemical and biological bombs against innocent Iranians, he was seen as a hero, not only for the US but also for the allied governments. But when he turned his back on them, he became a very undesirable person. When India was a close ally of communist Russia, Pakistan became the most favoured country for the United States. When the cold war was over, and India became the friend of the US, Pakistan became the least favoured state. Now, you need Pakistan again to fight against the Taliban, the military government of Pakistan has become very desirable to the US government once more. As far the people and the governments are concerned, nothing changed. The values, culture, religion, norms, everything has remained the same. What has changed is the short-term need of the USA. This means that the short-term needs of United States determine the criteria for what is terrorism and what is not terrorism. What is likable and what is not likable. Is this fair?

American citizens and installations have been under more terrorist attacks from the South American drug Mafia than from any other Middle Eastern linked attacks (excluding the September 11 attacks). More than 80% of all terrorist attacks on US citizens and installations have come from South American terrorist groups. There are terrorist groups in the USA, Europe and Australia such as White Supremacists, Jewish extremists, IRA, Red Army, etc. In Asia and Africa, there are terrorist groups like Shev Sinha in India, the Tamil Tigers in Sri Lanka, and the Red Army in Japan. Are there any plans to capture and punish these terrorist groups as well?

Imagine for a moment that those terrorists who attacked the WTC and the Pentagon on September 11 had carried out these attacks on non-US interests somewhere in Africa, the Middle East, Asia, Russia, or South America instead of New York and Washington DC. Would the government of the United States have reacted the same way as it is reacting now? Terrorism is terrorism, whether it is carried out in the USA or anywhere else. Russian forces have demolished entire cities in Chechnya and killed thousands of innocent civilians. Israeli forces daily demolish houses and kill innocent Palestinians – Christians and Muslims. The Indian Army has converted the entire state of Jammu and Kashmir in a high security jail and killed thousands of innocent civilians. Is this not terrorism? Are these not crimes against humanity?

Mr. President,

In my humble opinion, the war against terrorism will NOT be successful unless the US government is honest and fair with all humanity. American forces may be able to suppress terrorism and its causes temporarily, but they will not be able to eliminate or minimize terrorism unless the government of the USA adopts a simple principle. This principle should not change with each change in the successive American governments. The principle is:

"You should like for others what you like for yourself"

Since the American society wants to enjoy the freedom of choosing their lifestyle and their governments, please let the people of the third world countries be free to choose their lifestyles, governments, social, economic and political policies as well.

We must have a fixed definition of terrorism. It must not change based upon US needs. We must distinguish between freedom fighters and terrorists. The USA, being the champion of the free world, should support the freedom movements all over the world. If the people in East Timor can get independence from Indonesia, and the entire United Nations supports their struggle, why can Palestine, Kashmir and Chechnya not get their independence on the same grounds? Independence movements in Palestine, Kashmir and Chechnya are not terrorist movements. As Americans themselves once fought against the colonialism of British rule, they should understand the pain and suffering of freedom fighters. If these movements for national freedom are routinely treated as terrorist movements, this will create a major roadblock in fighting against terrorism.

The best way for resolving these issues of freedom is to use the democratic principles of freedom and choice in Kashmir, Palestine, Chechnya and other places in the world. Let the United Nations hold referendums in the areas where the movements of freedom are ongoing, and let the people decide what they want. This will eliminate reasons for violence and make this world a better, peaceful place. Let this "Operation Endeavoring Freedom" bring freedom for all oppressed people on the face of earth. Please remove all sanctions against the innocent people of Iraq and let them enjoy life as well.

Another important thing is that the United States government should not keep making the same mistake as they did in the case of Saddam Hussain. The Northern Alliance in Afghanistan is as hard-liner as the Taliban. I never agreed with the Taliban style of governing the country. In my opinion, some portions of their style of government are very un-Islamic and a disgrace to the Muslim community, but the Northern Alliance is worse than the Taliban. I do appreciate the $320 million food aid to Afghanis, but I am afraid that America may give them food with one hand, while the other hand may fire the bullet aimed at their throat. Please do not further destroy an already destroyed country. Afghanis have been oppressed by Russians and by their own fellow Afghanis. Why does America want to get its hands dirty by getting involved in this oppression? Please use peaceful means to capture terrorists. War will bring more chaos, destruction and killings to the world.

Finally, as an active Muslim member of the North American community, I founded the first anti-terrorist, non-governmental Muslim organization called "Muslims Against Terrorism" (M.A.T.) in 1999 in Calgary, Alberta, Canada. Now, MAT has members in more than 13 countries, including the USA and they are all working towards one goal: to make this world a peaceful place for everyone. Next year, MAT will be organizing an International conference on Counter Terrorism and we would like you to attend this conference in Canada. I will send you the details soon.

Thank you very much.

****

Date: September 12, 2011

The Right Hon. Stephen Harper

Prime Minister of Canada
Parliament Hill
Ottawa, Ontario, Canada
K1A 0A4

The Right Hon. Stephen Harper,

Your recent statements during an interview on the CBC, regarding how "Islamicism" is a threat to Canada, are misleading and confusing. It seems that your understanding of "Islamicism" and "Islamic Terrorism" is based upon the threats that Canada and the rest of the world are presently facing from fanatics and terrorists who call themselves Muslims. Is Islam the only religion facing this problem or have other religions had this problem, and continue to have it in the present as well? There are fanatics and extremists in every faith. They are the threat to Canada and to civil society.

The Islamic Supreme Council of Canada, Muslims Against Terrorism and ISCC affiliated mosques, fully support any effort that protects Canada and the Canadians from any threat. We support the Canadian government in countering threats to our country. However, your selection of words for identifying the threat was neither correct nor wise. In fact, the words "Islamicism" and "Islamic Terrorism" are misleading and completely inaccurate. These words actually help the terrorists in their propaganda of hate and spreading misinformation to non-Muslims about our faith. These words divide Canadians and harm our interfaith relationships.

How can you call something "Islamic" which has been repeatedly condemned and declared by overwhelming majority of Muslim scholars un-Islamic? Terrorism, extremism, fanaticism, violence and suicide bombings have been declared unlawful (haraam) and criminal in our holy book, the Qur'an, by our Prophet Muhammad (PBUH), by all early scholars of Islam and by the overwhelming majority of the current scholars of Islam. What else you need from Muslims, Mr. Prime Minister?

In January, 2010 more than twenty-eight Canadian and the American Imams affiliated with the Islamic Supreme Council of Canada issued a Fatwa declaring that any attack on Canada and the United States will be considered attack on Islam and Muslims? Around the world hundreds of prominent Muslim scholars have issued their own Fatwas declaring suicide bombings and terrorism to be criminal, and absolutely un-Islamic actions. The ISCC and many other Muslim organizations and mosques are doing their best to educate Muslim youth and elders to stay away from fanatics and extremists. I walked across Canada in 2008 and led the Multi-Faith Walk Against Violence. During the seven months of my walk, I met thousands of Muslims and non-Muslim Canadians, and raised awareness about the dangers of violence and terrorism. The ISCC holds weekly and monthly programs in various Canadian mosques across the country to help new immigrants in integrating with the mainstream Canadian society. We have made some progress but we have a long way to go. What else you want us to do Mr. Harper? Please let us know.

Mr. Harper, we promise you that we will do exactly what you want us to do, but for the sake of Jesus Christ (whom you say you love very much) please don't link Islam with any "ism" or "ist". There is no such thing as "Islamicism" OR "Islamists". Muslims do not create any link of Islam with any "ism" OR "ist". Our faith does not even recognize these links. Why are you trying to create such a link? We respect your religion. We do not associate your religion with any fanatic or terrorist. Why did you link Islam with fanatics and the terrorists? I do not see anywhere in the Canadian legal code that the Prime Minister of Canada can also define people's faiths. We know our faith very well, and we do not find fascism, fanaticism, extremism, terrorism, radicalism and hate for anyone in our faith.

Mr. Harper, Islam, a religion of 1.6 billion people, is not a monolithic religion. There are thousands of groups, cultures, ethnicities, several sects and denominations within the Muslims.

Any fanatic, extremist or terrorist who uses Islamic teachings to propagate violence against any Canadian must be identified with the "SECT" or group, or organization, or country of citizenship or birth. It's not difficult to find out the sectarian or group affiliation of a terrorist.

Once again, the Islamic Supreme Council of Canada, its affiliate organizations and mosques extend you and our government full support in defending Canada and Canadians. Please be assured that the Canadian Muslims are doing their best to watch out for any threats. We work very closely with our local law-enforcement agencies. We report any potential threat to them.

Mr. Prime Minister, we are all human and we do make mistakes. You made a mistake by linking Islam with terrorism and radicalism. It would be a very honourable action if you would kindly apologize to the Canadian Muslims for choosing poorly worded statements and retract your words. You are our Prime Minister, too, and we respect you. As voters, tax payers and law-abiding citizens of Canada we have the right to ask you to do the right thing. Please retract your words.

May God bless you and protect our country Canada from all evils. Amen

Thanks

****

September 25, 2001

Open Letter to the Muslim Brothers & Sisters Living in Muslim Countries

Dear Brothers and Sisters, Assalam-o-Alaikum,

I would like to warn you about the next western media campaign against Muslims regarding the treatment of Christian minorities living in Muslim countries, and at the same time remind you about our very Islamic duties with respect to the rights of minorities in Muslim countries. As we all realize, this is a critical period in the world's history. The terrorists who attacked the WTC and the Pentagon on September 11 were not only a few people who hijacked the planes, destroyed buildings and killed thousands of people in New York and Washington, D.C. It seems that these attacks were very carefully designed and planned. The people who planned these attacks knew that there would be a backlash against Muslims after these attacks. Thorough these attacks, they also wanted to destroy some Muslim countries and create animosity between Christians and Muslims. **We must not fall into this trap**. Yesterday, the CBC did broadcast a news item about the Christian minorities in Pakistan. Although, the news did not include any specific complaint, by now, we all know how the western media tries hard to put Muslims and Islam into a bad light. At present, the world media is focused on Pakistan. We all know very well that it is very difficult for the western media to find any positive thing about Muslims and Islam, they will try to find something they can sensationalize and present on the media in order to create animosity against Muslims. They will find some small incidents and sensationalize them. We know that the western media is influenced by some interest groups that do not want God loving people, Muslims and Christians, to live together peacefully.

We are living in a very different world from any time in the past. Just a few decades ago, the world was very much divided on religious and ethnic lines. This may still be true for Muslim countries. There have been no major changes in the demographics of Muslim countries but the demographics of Christian countries have significantly changed. Muslims have been migrating to Europe, North America and, Australia by the millions. Islam is the second largest religion in Europe, North

America and Australia. Muslims are the largest religious minority in these three continents. There are more than 10 million Muslims in North America alone, and they are increasing day by day.

On the other hand, unfortunately, the situation in Muslim countries is not good. Most of the governments in Muslim countries are very autocratic and dictator governments. These governments have been forced upon the people. This creates a sense of helplessness among the people, whether they are in the majority or the minority. Most of the governments in Muslim countries do not follow Islamic laws. Governments use Islam, when needed, in order to protect the rulers and their un-Islamic policies. Since, we do not have true Islamic laws providing complete protection for minorities, implemented in most of the Muslim countries it has become each individual Muslim's responsibility to protect his or her non-Muslim neighbours. As you may know, Islam has very protective laws for the non-Muslim minorities living in an Islamic State.

It is our duty as Muslims to make sure that the Christians and other non-Muslims are safe in Muslim countries. Our beloved Prophet Muhammad (PBUH) not only preached, but proved through his conduct that he always helped those who were oppressed. On many occasions when a dispute arose between a Muslim and a non-Muslim and the Prophet (PBUH) found that the non-Muslim was right, he made the decision in favour of the non-Muslim. That's the way the Companions of the Prophet Muhammad (PBUH) ruled. Justice is the most fundamental requirement of an Islamic state. I am sure as we, Muslim minority living in the western world follow the laws of the land, the non-Muslim minority also respects the laws of the Muslim countries. If we want to get justice and peace for ourselves we must treat others, Muslims and non-Muslims, with justice and peace as well.

It is our duty, as Muslims and Christians, to standup against those who are oppressors and want to carry out crusades against innocent people. May Allah help us. Ameen.

Thanks

****

Date: June 25, 2005

H.E. Kofi A. Anaan

Secretary General

The United Nations

New York, USA

H. E. Kofi A. Anaan,

Muslims Against Terrorism (MAT) was founded in Calgary, Alberta, Canada in 1998. The main objective of MAT is to create awareness about the dangers of violence and terrorism. The tragedy of 9/11 brought an increased focus on MAT, and this small Calgary based organization spread rapidly all over the world. We now have chapters in Canada, the USA, the UK, the Netherlands, Pakistan, Australia, Malaysia, Singapore and several other countries. MAT also works with other organizations to promote tolerance and peace in the communities.

Your Excellency, we know that the United Nations recognizes and honours the victims of various genocides and holocausts, including the holocaust and genocide of Jews, Christians, Aboriginals, and several other communities. However, we are very surprised that neither the United Nations, nor any other world body officially recognizes the Muslim victims of various Holocausts and Genocides.

In 2002, MAT and several other Muslim organizations declared **July 15 as a "Muslims Holocaust and Genocide emembrance Day".** Please allow me to give you some of the highlights of Holocausts and Genocides perpetrated specifically upon Muslims.

The first Holocaust against Muslims was carried out by the crusaders. On Friday, July 15, 1099 the crusaders captured Jerusalem and murdered thousands of Muslims. More than 70, 000 dead bodies of Muslim children and women were found in the Mosque of Omar in Jerusalem alone.

There have been several other Holocausts and genocides of Muslims;

1. Genghis Khan and his forces killed more than a million Muslims during the occupation of what is now Iraq and neighboring areas in 1258.

2. Thousands of Muslims were killed or forced to change religion by Spanish Crusaders in South America

3. More than a million Muslims were killed or displaced by the Spanish and other European extremists during the rebellion against the Ottoman Empire.

4. More than 3 million Muslims were killed or displaced by the European colonial powers during and after the occupation of Muslim countries after World Wars I and II.

5. More than 5 million Muslims were killed or displaced by the Tsars of Russia

6. More than a million Muslims were killed or displaced by Communist Government of Russia

7. More than 1/2 million Muslims were killed or displaced in East European countries while the various communist governments were in power in these countries.

8. More than 1.5 million Muslims have been killed in China, Cambodia, Vietnam, and other Far East countries since the World War II.

9. More than 1/2 million Muslims have been killed or displaced in Burma since World War II.

10. More than 1/2 million Muslims have been killed in India and Kashmir since 1947

11. More than 1/2 million Muslims were killed by Serbs and Croats in Bosnia during early 90s.

12.   More than 100,000 Muslims were killed in Kosovo and Albania during mid-90s.

13.   More than 5 million Muslims have been killed or displaced in Palestine since 1948

14.   More than 6 million Muslims were killed or displaced as a result of the Russian occupation of Afghanistan

15.   Since their independence from the colonial powers, thousands of Muslims have been killed in their own countries by secular governments backed by Western governments.

16.   Currently, hundreds of innocent civilians are being killed by the American forces in Iraq and Afghanistan.

We would like to request that you declare July 15 as a "Muslims Holocaust and Genocide Remembrance Day". We are also urging all fellow human beings to remember the Muslim victims of so many Holocausts and Genocides on July 15.

The first holocaust of Muslims took place on Friday, July 15, 1099 by the hands of Crusaders in Palestine.

Articles

Date: November 21, 2015

Nine Points Guarantee – The Elimination of Terrorism

These nine points are practical, real and achievable. They just need the will of all governments especially, especially the NATO governments to sincerely and honestly implement them.

1. It should be illegal to recruit, fund, train, arm and support civilians in fights against their own governments. No government should directly or indirectly get involved in toppling the governments of other countries by using the local or foreign civilians.

2. All Muslim countries, especially Saudi Arabia, must ban all Imams and other religious leaders, and their literature condemning fellow Muslims on the basis of sectarian differences among Islamic schools of thought. Saudi Arabia must stop supporting and exporting the Wahhabism/Salafism within its own borders, and other parts of the world. Wahhabism / Salafism is the root cause of sectarian-based violence among Muslims. Muslims of all sects must be allowed to practice their beliefs and traditions openly in all Muslim countries, even in Saudi Arabia and Iran.

3. All Muslim countries must declare calling a fellow Muslims of other sects "Kafir", "Mushrik" or "Bidatee" (non-Muslim or sinners). Using these designations as an excuse for legal or extra-legal persecution should be declared a punishable crime according to International Law. Inciting hatred towards Christians, Jews and people of other religions should be a punishable crime as well. Disagreements among religions and sects should create opportunities for dialogue instead of excuses for hate and violence.

4. Joining supporting funding or sympathizing with any terrorist organization must be illegal in all countries.

5. All Western countries, especially the United States, must immediately stop interfering in the affairs of Muslim countries. Any support or aid to poor countries must not be conditional, based on demands and directives (from the donor) on how to run the country, except to assure that the aid is not misused.

6. All Western governments, especially the United States government, must immediately stop their one-sided, unjust policies in the Middle East and elsewhere. An independent secure and safe Palestine must be established immediately based upon the borders of Israel set before 1967. Both Israel and Palestine must be treated equally and justly. The peaceful freedom movements must be supported in all parts of the world, including Palestine, Kashmir, Chechnya, Russian Federation, etc.

7. Islamophobia, anti-Semitism, anti-Christian propaganda and hate mongering against any faith group, must be declared illegal. Western media must stop immediately linking terrorism with Islam and Muslims. Designations like, "Islamic Terrorism", "Muslim Terrorists", "Islamists" or "Jihadist" are essentially fallacious. A truly informed public requires that the western media accurately identify terrorists with their respective "Fanatic sectarian beliefs", their organizations, or their countries of origin. Do not automatically link the entire faith of Islam, or the word, "Jihad" with terrorism. In western countries there are fanatic Christian and Jewish TV evangelists who openly spread hate in the public media against Islam and Muslims. They must be stopped immediately.

8. Respect the human rights of all citizens equally and fairly. Freedom of speech, freedom of religion and freedom of lifestyle must be available to all citizens equally. However, the use of freedom of speech to incite hatred towards any segment of the society must be a punishable crime. Muslims must not be held responsible for the crimes of ISIS, the Taliban, Al-Qaeda or any

violent Muslim individual suffering from mental illness, just like Christians are not held responsible for the crimes of KKK, the Aryan Nation, Nazis or similarly mentally-ill Christian individuals.

9.   The rights of all minorities in all countries must be respected and protected. Muslim governments must protect Christian and other minorities in Muslim countries. Western countries must stop threatening their Muslim citizens with punishment for the crimes of terrorists who call themselves Muslims. The racism and violence against Muslim minorities in Burma, India, Europe, North America, Australia, and other parts of the world, and against the Christian minorities in Pakistan, Iraq, Syria, Egypt, among others, must be stopped.

NOTE FOR MUSLIMS: It is the requirement of Islam for every Muslim to be a loyal, faithful and law-abiding citizen of the country he/she lives in. In Islam there is no superiority based upon gender, colour, language, ethnicity, etc. Better among us is the one who is more righteous among us. In Islam, it is the right of every human, Muslim or non-Muslim, to get justice and help when in need. In Islam, it is the right of every human, Muslim *or* non-Muslim for his/her life and property to be respected and protected. The core principle of Islam is the "Sanctity of life". The foundation of Islam is "love and sacrifice". The goal of life is to obey Allah and His Messenger Muhammad (PBUH). The purpose of life is to serve Allah's creation. In Islam the rights of people are as important, in some cases more important, than the rights of Allah (God). Hate, misogyny, violence, drugs, revenge, arrogance, ignorance and discrimination are un-Islamic acts. A believer's heart cannot have both; the love for Allah and hate for His creation. A soft and tender heart is the identity of a Muslim. May the peace and the blessings of Allah on the entire creation of Allah (God). Amen.

Live and let the others live. Do not abandon yours and do not attack others' beliefs.

****

Islamic Shari'a – A Blessing or a Burden

Recently an article was published in the Calgary Sun regarding the use of Islamic Shari'a in the dispute resolution process for Canadian Muslim families under the Arbitration Act of Ontario. Before I respond to that article let me briefly explain what Shari'a is, and what it is not.

The Arabic word Shari'a means, the way of "laws, rules, regulations". In other words, Shari'a is the code of conduct for Muslims. The laws of Shari'a are mainly based upon the teachings of the Holy Qur'an, the sayings (Hadith) and practices (Sunnah) of Prophet of Islam, Muhammad (PBUH). In order to address the issues and problems of future times, Shari'a has several other sources as well, such as the interpretation of the Qur'an and Hadith by the family and the companions of the Prophet Muhammad (PBUH), the rulings of Islamic jurists (e.g. Faqih or Mujtahid). But no jurist has the authority to overrule the Qur'an and the Prophet Muhammad (peace be upon him)

Islam is not merely a religion. It is a normal, natural way of life, and views intolerance, racism and violence as abnormal behaviour. The purpose of Islam is to create a very strong ethical and spiritual society on earth. In order to create such a society, Islam provides a complete road map. This road map is called "Shari'a".

From the early 7th century until the 18th century, Islamic countries fully enforced the Islamic Shari'a. That might be the reason why the Muslim nations were the superpowers of the world of that time. Currently, there is not a single Islamic state where Shari'a is enforced in its full and pure form. Only bits and pieces of Shari'a have been enforced, and this is what confuses many people.

The Calgary Sun article, "Weird notions, Intolerance isn't acceptable — even in the name of 'tolerance'," was a very misleading article. It is obvious that the writer either did not know the principles of Islamic Shari'a, which he should have found out before writing the article in the newspaper, or he was purposely trying to mislead Canadians.

Let me analyze his article. The writer wrote:

" Like most Canadians, I know little about the Muslim legal system called "sharia," but from what we hear about places such as Nigeria, Sudan, Afghanistan and East Timor where it is fully enforced, I don't like it."

The above statement is false and extremely misleading. In East Timor, Shari'a was never enforced. In fact, past and present governments of Indonesia never enforced Shari'a. In order to please Christians, the dictator Suharto removed Islam as the official religion of Indonesia.

Shari'a has never been fully enforced in Nigeria, either. In a few provinces of Nigeria, a fragmented form of "Shari'a" has been enforced.

The version of "Shari'a" imposed by the Taliban in Afghanistan was never accepted by the overwhelming majority of Islamic jurists. Nor is Shari'a fully enforced in Sudan. The government of Sudan has "Islamized" some of the laws, but this is no way close to the full implementation of Shari'a.

The writer wrote:

" In some countries, sharia requires women to stay indoors, or walk around together wearing tents so no one can see them. A right to abortion? There are places where women would settle for the right to drive a car."

It is evident that the writer is completely ignorant about Shari'a. Islamic Shari'a cannot be customized for specific countries. Islamic Shari'a does not require women to stay indoors. Islamic Shari'a does not require women to wear tents. Islamic Sharia does not require that no one should see a woman. No aspect of Islamic Shari'a prevents or disallows women the right to drive a car. What Islamic Shari'a requires from both men and women is modest dress. In Catholicism, nuns are enjoined to wear modest dress. Islam requires that all women should dress modestly, and attempt to be more pious - not just the select few. Islam wants everyone to be pious as a means to better society. What is bad about this?

The writer wrote:

"The Law Times legal journal reported in its Nov. 25 edition that on Oct. 21, a legal conference of Muslims in Etobicoke, Ont., elected a 30-member council. The council will establish a judicial tribunal to be known as the Islamic Institute of Civil Justice (Canada). And the IICJ will dispense Muslim justice under the Ontario Arbitration Act."

"The obvious danger of a sharia arbitration system is it will not be voluntary. A Muslim who opts for a secular court instead of the local kangaroo arbitrator would be expelled from the Muslim community. If you are a newly arrived mother who can't speak English and can't make a living, how realistic is this?"

I am one of the founding members of IICJ. I was the MC of that gathering on Oct. 21, 2003. Without having the knowledge of the decisions made in that open meeting, the writer has apparently made an attempt to create fear among his fellow Canadians, and to mislead them by fabricating rumors.

The writer is wrong to say that, "The obvious danger of a Shari'a arbitration system is it will not be voluntary". This statement is false. What proof does the writer have that it will not be voluntary? It is completely voluntary. Secondly, Muslims do not have the power to expel other Muslims from the community. Thirdly, calling an arbitrator licensed according to Canadian law, a purveyor of "Kangaroo justice", is an insult to the profession of arbitrators in Canada.

While English may, indeed, pose a problem for new immigrants in Canadian courts, English or French will not be a problem for IICJ because we will have access to the wealth of languages of most of the Muslim world. IICJ will be able to help Canadian courts with their language needs.

The clear objective of IICJ is to use the existing arbitration laws to help Muslim families to resolve their family disputes, and help Muslim business people to resolve their business disputes. Criminal justice is not a part of this particular system of arbitration. I think the writer should read the Ontario arbitration act first before hurling wild accusations at Muslims. In reality, arbitration cannot be applied in all types of disputes. Arbitration laws deal with a very limited area of dispute resolution.

The writer wrote:

"Arbitrators should be required to apply Canadian legal principles and values, not imported ones. That way, a Muslim could still be an arbitrator, and Muslims could still go to him for justice. But his decision would have to rest on Canadian judicial principles, or the arbitrator would be delicensed and the loser given recourse to the courts."

It, in fact, is the mandate of IICJ to resolve disputes *in accordance with Canadian laws* by using the principles of dispute resolution of Islamic Shari'a. There is no conflict between the Canadian arbitration laws and the dispute resolution principles of Islamic Shari'a. That is the beauty of Islamic Shari'a and the Canadian arbitration laws - which may not be known to the writer.

The writer wrote:

"This country is getting genuinely weird. In the cause of tolerance, we let Muslims establish their intolerant legal system within our own".

In my opinion, this statement is, itself, very intolerant and hateful towards Islam and Muslims. Muslims in North America are concerned about the rise of racism in North American society. Since the 9/11 tragedy, many so-called seasonal experts on Islam have accused Islam and Muslims of being an intolerant religion, and an intolerant community. They use the tragedy of 9/11 to create misunderstanding and hate among the citizens of this world. As civilized citizens, we must oppose this movement of hate and violence. After 9/11, hate crimes against Muslims have significantly increased. When a reader reads misleading articles designed to instill a sense of fear and uncertainty among the public, the possibility exists for this reader to be influenced by the opinion of the writer and, consequently, inspired to commit hate crimes against Muslims in Canada. Who will be responsible for such crimes?

How could Canadians allow an intolerant legal system to be a part of the Canadian legal system? Canadian Muslims would be the first to oppose such an action. A few centuries ago, under a fully enforced system of Shari'a, Muslims, Jews and Christians lived side by side in Morocco, Algeria, Tunisia, Bosnia, Albania, and other nations. Let me ask some questions. Should we blame the Christian faith for the genocide of Muslims committed by the crusaders during the 10th century? Should we blame Jesus Christ (PBUH) for the crimes committed in his name by the Christian missionaries in South America four centuries ago? Should we blame Christianity for the nuclear bombs dropped by the US forces on Hiroshima and Nagasaki? Should we blame Jesus Christ (PBUH) for the Holocaust of 6 million Jews committed by Christians? Should we blame Christians for the kidnapping and murder of innocent people in South America by the Christian drug Mafia? Certainly not. Similarly, neither should the Prophet Muhammad (PBUH), nor the Islamic Shari'a be blamed for the behaviour of any extremist that uses Islam for his/her own personal gains. The current chaos in Muslim countries is not because of Shari'a. It is because of the absence of Shari'a.

In Canada, church and state are separate. The Canadian parliament is the legislative authority. The Supreme Court of Canada is the final authority on interpreting laws - a very simple and straightforward system. The government and the people respect the constitution and the system. However, the current situation of Muslim countries is very complex and corrupt. Currently, no Muslim country has the implementation of Islamic laws (Shari'a) in its pure and complete form. There are several sources of laws:

- The inherited laws and regulations from the various colonial eras;

- The rulers (most of them military dictators);

- The parliament (if it exists);

- The Islamic Shari'a (used as a scapegoat).

The lack of democracy and sense of accountability in Muslim countries gives a free hand to rulers and/or governments to arbitrarily reward or punish a person as they see fit? When a poor person, or a bitter opponent commits a crime, the government employs, or in reality misuses the Shari'a in order to quell any possibility of public opposition. No one wants to be seen as raising a voice against religion, so Shari'a ends up getting used as a scapegoat.

When a powerful and rich person, or someone close to the ruler's family and friends commits a crime, then the rulers decides uses his own discretion in selectively applying the laws - Shari'a or other laws.

Most of the time, Shari'a is completely ignored when the for the rich and powerful are involved. The media barely covers this dark side of Muslim rulers, while tending to sensationalize other cases. When a Nigerian court sentences a poor woman to death, it becomes headline news; meanwhile, the corruption of Muslim rulers of the country involved is hardly ever reported on. The abuse of Shari'a by the rulers and the courts in Muslim countries continues to create confusion among westerners.

On the other hand, a small minority of Islamic clergy, have developed their own interpretations of Islam, sometimes disregarding the actual teachings of the Prophet Muhammad (PBUH), and the holy Qur'an in favour of cultural and tribal traditions, and later innovations. The Prophet Muhammad (PBUH) implemented Shari'a after he purified the hearts and minds of the society (the inner side of a person). He implemented Shari'a after he made sure that no one would sleep hungry in the Islamic state. When he (PBUH) asked women to dress modestly, he also asked men to dress modestly and lower their gaze. Sincerity, honesty, purity and economic independence is the pre-requisite of Shari'a. Before implementing Shari'a, Muslim governments and jurists must make sure that every citizen of their country has food, shelter and clothing. Shari'a cannot be implemented on empty stomachs. A person who is going to die because of hunger can steal food, and no one has the right to cut off his hands. This is what Shari'a says. If a woman is raped by a man, the man should be punished, not the woman. The so-called "honour killings" have no basis in Islamic Shari'a, but represent a cruel custom carried over from ignorant times. The rights of women and non-Muslim minorities are completely protected by Islamic Shari'a. There should be no doubt about this. Therefore, Islamic Shari'a is a blessing not a burden. The corrupt rulers of Muslim countries and their "own" justice systems are the burdens and it is they that must be removed.

The freedom to have differences of opinion is the beauty of a democratic society, but false accusations towards a segment of the society should not be accepted by anyone.

Prof. Imam Syed Badiuddin Soharwardy

Syed Badiuddin Soharwardy was born to a highly respected religious family in Karachi, Pakistan. He immigrated to Canada with his family from Saudi Arabia in 1995. His father, Allama Syed Muhammad Riazuddin Soharwardy (May Allah shower His blessings upon him), was a famous Islamic scholar, a school teacher, a poet and the Imam of Jamia Bughdadi Masjid, Martin Road, Karachi, where he established the Dar-ul-Aloom Soharwardia. Imam Soharwardy's grandfather, Allama Syed Muhammad Jalaluddin Chishty (May Allah shower His blessings upon him), was the Grand Mufti of Kashmir (Baramula). Allama Jalaluddin Chishty later migrated to Amritsar (India) where he served as the head of the Dar-ul-Aloom Nizamiah Sirajiah and the Imam of a Mosque. The internationally renowned Naat Khawn Qari Syed Fasihuddin Soharwardy and the famous Imam in Karachi, Pakistan, Allama Syed Ejazuddin Soharwardy are his younger brothers.

Imam Syed Soharwardy and his ancestors are among the direct descendants of Prophet Muhammad (peace be upon him). Through Imam Ja'far us-Sadiq (May Allah's peace upon him), Imam Soharwardy's lineage reaches to Sayyidatunnisa (leader of all women) Hazrat Fatimah Binte Muhammad ibn Abdullah (PBUH), the wife of Ameer ul Mo'mineen Sayyidna Imam Ali (May Allah's peace upon him). His ancestors migrated from Syria to Iran where they settled in the Zarrin, or Zarrindasht area in Asfahan province. During the 1200s A.H. a famous Sufi scholar, Hazrat Syed Bahauddin Ziryani (May Allah be pleased with him) was born to this family. Later, Hazrat Syed

Bahauddin Ziryani migrated to, and settled in Kashmir (India) where after five generations, Allama Mufti Syed Muhammad Jalaluddin Chishty (May Allah be pleased with him) was born.

Imam Soharwardy received his early Islamic education from his father, teacher and Murshad (spiritual guide) in the traditional Islamic Madrasah at the Jamia Bughdadi Masjid, Martin Road, Karachi, Pakistan. Later, he graduated from Dar-ul-Aloom Soharwardia, Karachi. Mr. Soharwardy also earned a Bachelor of Arts degree in Islamic Studies from the University of Karachi.

In addition to his Islamic education, Mr. Soharwardy has four Engineering degrees: an Associate Electrical Engineering diploma from the Jinnah Polytechnic Institute, Karachi, a Bachelor of Engineering (Electrical) from N.E.D. University of Engineering & Technology, Karachi, a Master of Science in Industrial Management Engineering from the New Jersey Institute of Technology, Newark, NJ, USA and a Master of Engineering in Project Management from the University of Calgary, Alberta, Canada. His Ph.D. in Project Management at the University of Bournemouth, UK remains incomplete, as his extremely busy schedule defending Islam and the Muslim community has not allowed him the time for this. Syed Badiuddin Soharwardy's work as an IT consultant is what pays his bills. His community and religious work is 100% volunteer work. He charges no fee for his Imam-related work and lectures.

Imam Syed Soharwardy was appointed as a teacher at Dar-ul-Aloom Soharwardia where he taught various subjects in the field of Islamic studies. Later, he also served as the assistant Imam and Khateeb at Jamia Bughdadi Masjid, Martin Road (1972- 1984). Imam Soharwardy has lectured in Pakistan, the USA and Saudi Arabia at various universities and institutes for over 12 years.

Prof. Soharwardy is the founder of Muslims Against Terrorism (MAT). He founded MAT in Calgary in January, 1998 quite some time before the tragedy of 9/11. After the 9/11 tragedy, MAT spread to several countries around the world. Imam Soharwardy is also the founder of the Islamic Supreme Council of Canada (ISCC). The ISCC was founded in the year 2000 in

Calgary and has now evolved into a national Canadian Islamic organization with chapters in Surrey, Calgary, Edmonton, Saskatoon, Winnipeg, Toronto, Mississauga, Brampton and Montreal. He has written several articles and Op-Ed columns in the Calgary Herald and other newspapers on various Islamic and social topics. He has authored three books Eid-Milad-un-Nabi (PBUH), Islamic Worship (Ebadaat) and Defeating Hate. His next book is on the root cause of Muslim division. Mr. Soharwardy has lectured hundreds of gatherings in Pakistan, the USA, UK and Canada on various topics of Islamic faith.

In 2008, Imam Soharwardy led the *Multi-Faith Walk Against Violence*. He walked more than 6500 km. from Halifax to Victoria to raise awareness about violence in society, including domestic violence, animal abuse, elder abuse and terrorism. To date, he is the only Canadian Muslim who has walked across the Canada. Imam Soharwardy mortgaged his own house to fund his milestone Walk.

Imam Soharwardy has established / leads the following mosques/Islamic centres across the country.

1. Jamia Masjid Gunbad-e-Khizra (Green Dome) Mosque, Calgary NE, Alberta
2. Al Makkah Calgary Islamic Centre, Alberta
3. Jamia Riyadhul Jannah, Mississauga, Ontario
4. Jamia Riyadhul Jannah, Edmonton, Alberta
5. Jamia Masjid Noor-e-Madinah, Montreal, Quebec
6. Spiritual Society Masjid, Toronto, Ontario
7. Al Tawakkal Musallah, Toronto, Ontario
8. Aisha Masjid Niagra Falls, Ontario
9. Jamia Masjid Aulia Allah, Surrey, British Columbia
10. Jamia Masjid Aisha, Cornwall, Ontario
11. Jamia Riyadhul Jannah, Saskatoon, Saskatchewan
12. Jamia Riyadhul Jannah, Winnipeg, Manitoba
13. Sayyidah Zainab (AS) Muslim Community Centre, Toronto (in planning)

14. Sayyidah Fatemah (AS) Food Bank, Calgary, Alberta
15. Muslim Cemetery For South Edmonton, Alberta

Imam Soharwardy is the chairman of the board of directors for the following registered charities,

1. Al Madinah Calgary Islamic Assembly, Calgary, Alberta
2. Canadian Society of Peace and Relief, Mississauga, Ontario
3. Canadian Ministries For Islamic Learning Edmonton
4. Islamic Association of Western Canada, Surrey, B.C.
5. Muslim Council of Saskatchewan, Saskatoon, Saskatchewan

Imam Soharwardy led the efforts in uniting Canadian Imams and religious leaders to issue formal "Fatwas" (religious edicts) against the following:

1. The brutality and extremism of Taliban and Al-Qaeda in 2009. This was the first formally issued Fatwa in the world against the Taliban and Al-Qaeda's incorrect interpretation of Islam;

2. Terrorism against Canada and the United States in 2010. This was the first formal Fatwa in the world against the attacks on Canada and the United States;

3. Misogyny, honour killings and domestic violence in 2012;

4. Forced and underage marriages;

5. Radicalization and joining the Daesh (ISIS).

Imam Soharwardy appeared in front of the Canadian Senate's standing committee on National Defence and Security, and provided his views on the rise of extremism and terrorism among Muslim youth.

Imam Soharwardy actively participates in interfaith dialogues. Since the tragedy of 9/11 he has participated in more than 185 interfaith dialogues in various churches, synagogues, temples, community centres and institutions. This does not include interfaith dialogues he participates on monthly basis under various interfaith groups. For details please visit http://www.islamicsupremecouncil.com/interfaith-dialogues-and-islam-101-classes/. He initiated the Calgary Jewish-Muslim Council and co-founded it with Rabbi Shaul Osadchey. He brings Muslim, Jewish and Christian families together to share meals at Mosques, Synagogues and Churches. This grass roots work has been beneficial, not only in reducing the Islamophobia but in helping to build bridges and promote harmony in the Canadian society.

He is a very outspoken Canadian Muslim leader whose tireless efforts to stand up against radicalization, extremism and terrorism are known to the Canadian media and to his fellow Canadians.

Imam Soharwardy is a strong advocate of Islamic Tasawuf (Sufism) and believes that the world will be a better place for everyone, if we follow what the Prophet of Islam, Muhammad (peace be upon him) has said:

"You will not have faith unless you like for others what you like for yourself."

He believes that spiritual weakness in humans causes all manner of problems. Imam Soharwardy has the "Ijazah" in Soharwardy, Qadri and Chishti Sufi orders from his Murshad (spiritual guide), Allama Syed Muhammad Riazuddin Soharwardy, Qadri, Chishti (May Allah's blessings upon him). He is the Khalifah of his Murshad. His students and Murideen (disciples) have spread out all over the world.

Imam Soharwardy can be contacted at **Soharwardy@iscc.ca** or by telephone at (403)-831-6330, or at 416-994-5467, https://twitter.com/syedsoharwardy, https://www.facebook.com/SyedSoharwardy/

Further information can also be found at the following websites:

www.iscc.ca, www.m-a-t.org , www.worldsufimission.org , www.cspr.ca, www.amcia.org , www.sufitv.tv, www.jrjsk.ca, www.iawc.net, www.jrjedmonton.org, www.ccmic.ca